A Parent's Guide to Homeschooling:
The Complete Guide

"Homeschooling is a big family decision. If you want solid support, information, and imaginative help, I suggest that you carry Tamra Orr's book under your arm or sit with the family around the kitchen table and simply read it out loud."

—**Ashisha**, Editor,
Mothering Magazine

"Every new homeschooler should own this book! *A Parent's Guide to Homeschooling* answers the questions facing most new homeschoolers and presents them in a format that makes it easy to find the information you need. It includes contributions from many well known names in the homeschool community as well as other moms and dads who can speak from experience. Topped off by several appendices of resources, this book will provide everything you need to start your homeschooling journey."

—**Billy Greer**, FUN Books,
formerly the John Holt Bookstore

"Finally—a no-holds-barred introduction to homeschooling! Parents who are considering homeschooling their children will find this an encouraging reference guidebook, covering all the bases while offering plenty of experienced support and helpful resources. Tamra Orr's new book offers the experienced perspective of home-schooling's pioneering personalities, but also goes a step further and includes essays from homeschooling parents 'in the trenches,' providing real-life descriptions of how homeschooling works for a wide variety of families. Definitely a standout title in what has become a flood of homeschooling books hitting the market."

—**Helen Hegener**, Editor,
Home Education Magazine

"If you're curious about homeschooling—the fastest growing trend in education today—this comprehensive, easy-to-read Guide is the book to read. We highly recommend it."

—**Rebecca Kochenderfer**, Senior Editor,
Homeschool.com

"This easy to use and easy to read guide will help you make all the right choices for homeschooling your child."

—**Patrick Farenga**, author of
Teach your Own: The John Holt Guide to Homeschooling

parent's
guide
press

After Homeschool

Fifteen Homeschoolers Out in the Real World

Tamra Orr

los angeles, california
www.pgpress.com

**parent's
guide
press**

After Homeschool

Fifteen Homeschoolers Out in the Real World

LC
40
.DT5
2003

ISBN: 1-931199-30-2

This book, and all titles in the Parent's Guide series, are available for purposes of fund raising and educational sales to charity drives, fund raisers, parent or teacher organizations, schools, government agencies and corporations at a discount for purchases of more than 10 copies. Persons or organizations wishing to inquire should call Mars Publishing at 1-800-549-6646 or write to us at **sales@marspub.com**.

Please contact us at **parentsguides@marspub.com**

7   12   29   34   45   AA

Edwin E. Steussy, CEO and Publisher
Anna-Lisa Fay, Project Editor
Michael P. Duggan, Graphic Artist

PO Box 461730
Los Angeles CA 90046

parent's guide press

After Homeschool
Fifteen Homeschoolers Out In The Real World

Contents

After Homeschool
Fifteen Homeschoolers Out In The Real World

Foreword
by Grace Llewellyn

I'm so pleased this new collection of personal stories about older and grown up homeschoolers has come into print. Portraits such as these are deeply valuable and we need to see more of them available in various forms of media.

It seems there are three important questions any family or individual contemplating homeschooling should ask. Firstly: "In the broadest sense, what is possible and valuable in this realm of learning?" Secondly: "Who am I, and what might my personal qualities and dreams lead me to do and become?" And finally: "How are others growing outside of schools and other institutions?"

This book directly helps us answer this third question. Another way to answer it is to personally get to know homeschoolers, but on its own, this is tricky. Unless you get to *deeply* know a *wide variety* of homeschoolers — you may be misled because much of its nature is in its breadth and its huge realm of choice.

When I say "deeply?" I've observed that teenaged homeschoolers tend to downplay their activities. I'll never forget one of the times I facilitated a panel of teenagers who responded to an audience of parents (mostly of younger children) at a homeschooling conference. I knew the participants very well, and my jaw dropped when a parent would ask, for example: "What do you do during the day?" and a panelist replied: "Well, I sleep until noon or later, and then I mostly goof off until dinner," neglecting to point out that after dinner, he typically spent 8 hours working on his fantasy novel and learning computer programming. Other panelists also neglected to mention tidbits like a graphic design business, a band that had recently toured the state, etc. I've also witnessed incomplete accounting in other places where homeschoolers share information about themselves. For a variety of

Foreword

understandable reasons—not wanting to appear arrogant, not wanting to play into the too-common notion that homeschooling's validity depends on the academic or artistic stardom of its practitioners, and simply not categorizing many of their activities as noteworthy or "educational"—homeschoolers often paint a misleading picture of their own achievements.

And why "wide variety?" One of the best things about homeschooling is that the breadth of what's possible is staggeringly huge. There are as many ways to homeschool as there are people on this planet—more, in fact, because as the essays here show, an individual's or family's approach often changes significantly from one year to the next. Having access to a variety of stories, therefore, is really valuable. This way we can begin to understand the range of possible goals, activities, resources, products, subject areas, philosophical underpinnings, parental roles, and other issues.

Tamra Orr's collection does a comprehensive job of representing one particular aspect of the breadth of homeschooling, one I'd like to single out briefly. The public and the media, and consequently those first beginning to consider homeschooling, have often suffered from the misconception that there are basically two distinct camps of homeschoolers: fundamentalist Christians who use prepackaged curriculums and run a miniature school at home, and hippie eccentrics who are not conventionally religious and eschew any form of structure. And I do mean *suffer*, because to the degree that we view the homeschooling movement in this way, we miss out, at the very least, on the deep pleasure of knowing the rich truth. In my experience interacting with thousands of homeschoolers, this reductive (and often patronizing) polarized categorization is largely a myth, and I'm pleased that Tamra's book reveals some of the complexity that belies the myth. Gwen's story, for instance, in Chapter Two, gives a refreshingly unboxed view of what a homeschooler can be.

Foreword

It's easy to take for granted what we have, so I want to point out, those of us who got interested in homeschooling 15 or more years ago weren't lucky enough to have books like this one. I vividly recall my first reading of John Holt, one of the most influential inspirers of the homeschooling movement. It was very powerful to read his work and watch my understanding of learning quickly unravel and rebuild itself in a new shape. It was also very powerful to begin reading his magazine, *Growing Without Schooling*, which offered detailed reports from individual homeschoolers, and then to personally contact hundreds of these people who were practicing his ideas. But aside from *GWS*, a handful of exciting autobiographical books written by homeschooling families or individuals, and my own time-intensive personal research, I didn't have much access to stories. It's easier now, but still, a surprisingly small amount of literature has focused on the actual lives of older, or now adult, homeschoolers. So each new book on the subject is an important contribution.

Finally, the greatest potential and magic for all of us—homeschoolers, prospective homeschoolers, and everybody else, that homeschooling has to offer is not revealed through comparing it to other forms of education or even discussing it *as* a form of education, nor in pointing out and basking in the glory of its prodigies and super-achievers, but rather in investigating it as much as possible on its own terms and in the context of all of life. I really agree with Tami's definition of success—"you are happy, healthy, you love and are loved in return, and you are doing something fulfilling and meaningful with your time." Homeschooling can hugely facilitate those aspirations, and these portraits starkly reveal the joie d' vivre—the *success*—of their subjects.

Foreword

In this regard, like any good material on the actual lives of homeschoolers, this collection offers timeless, universal lessons. As a single adult without my own children, I am inspired completely apart from the question of my career, which is directly related to homeschooling, and in the hope that I may one day soon raise my own family of out-of-the-box explorers. I am also inspired to invent my life the way I want it to be and believe it can be and am reminded that so much more is possible than our various institutions and conventions lead us to believe. Just because most people in our society live, learn, love, communicate, work, play, and die within a narrow spectrum of behavior doesn't mean that any of us have to do so. This collection is a joyful affirmation that we can always start fresh and reach wide and there is always far more splendor to discover and create than we previously imagined.

Grace Llewellyn is author of The Teenage Liberation Handbook: How to Quit School and Get a Real Life and Education; coauthor of Guerrilla Learning: How to Give Your Kids a Real Education With or Without School and editor of Real Lives: Eleven Teenagers Who Don't Go to School, and Freedom Challenge: African American Homeschoolers, as well as the Founder and Director of the Not Back to School Camp

Chapter One

Where Do We Go From Here?

Let's face it—15 years ago, homeschoolers were all oddballs, neurotics, radicals or religious fanatics—at least, that's what people seemed to think. Today, the picture has changed. Instead of just a handful of those bizarre homeschoolers, more than a million families have chosen this educational option. That is a number that will only grow with time because parents are questioning everything from standards and quality of education to school safety. Now, when I inform people that our family is homeschooling, the reaction is an all-new (and usually improved) experience. Instead of raised eyebrows, furrowed brows and a look of disapproval, I usually hear: "Oh, my sister/neighbor/ coworker does that" or "I just read an article/heard a talk show/talked to my spouse about that!" Homeschooling is becoming well known and as more people like James Dobson, William Bennett or John Taylor Gatto begin to advocate—no, emphatically urge—parents to homeschool, it will most likely become more widespread.

After Homeschool
Fifteen Homeschoolers Out In The Real World

Chapter One

As homeschooling continues to grow and expand over the years, so does the literature that surrounds it. A continual line of books is being published to help parents learn everything from how to begin or what curriculum to use to what field trips can be taken or what to do about various possible learning disabilities. However, because the homeschooling movement is also still quite young, very little is known about this first generation of young adults who are emerging from years of home education and venturing out into the world. What are they doing with their lives? Are they successful? Are they happy? Do they get jobs or go to college? Do they grab the opportunity for life, liberty and the pursuit of happiness? How do they feel about missing football games, the prom or graduation? Do they feel they are missing out—or do they feel they're being exposed to other things? What about their parents? How did they ever cope with the teen years and the issues that come along with it?

Only relatively few books have focused on the different journeys and pathways this truly unique and emerging generation is taking (see resources for books by Linda Dobson, Cafi Cohen and Grace Llewellyn). For this reason, I was inspired to put pen to paper and write a book that fills a huge gap in the market and takes a close look at the lives of fifteen older homeschoolers and what they do with their time, lives, energy and passions.

The young people found here are not chosen because they just won yet another national spelling or geography bee or earned a perfect score on their SATs (although homeschoolers have done both) but because they are typical homeschoolers and everyday youths—from a variety of backgrounds, philosophies, families

Where Do We Go From Here?

and perspectives. Here you will read about secular and religious homeschoolers as well as structured and unstructured students. Some are doing school at home; some are unschooling; most are somewhere in between. Some have chosen the college option; some have not. They are here to share with the rest of the world what older homeschoolers are like and the incredible myriad of ways they approach the adult portions of their lives. They address some of the most common issues that people wonder about like socialization, future education and careers.

As I interviewed each one of them, however, I couldn't help but think that anyone who spent more than a few minutes talking to these young people would stop worrying about how they would turn out. Without exception, I found them all to be articulate, intelligent and very comfortable talking about their lives. Their stories can inspire and comfort parents who are wondering just how their homeschooled children will turn out some years down the road or they can help to educate those who are wondering what kind of people this new educational movement is going to create. I believe the portraits here will bring peace of mind to both groups of people as they see these young adults following different paths, yet all doing so with individuality, maturity and boundless imagination.

As a homeschooling mom myself, only one of my children has reached the teen years so far (see the chapter by Jasmine Orr for the inside scoop on her particular pathway) and it has been quite a journey for both of us. It has given me insight into not only her world and way of thinking, but by meeting and talking with her peers and the world of other homeschooling teens. It has

Chapter One

been fascinating to see the differences—and the similarities. These teens still grapple with many of the same issues as other teens—what to do in life, the confusion of hormones, vacillating between child and adult—but they often do so in a completely different manner. They have a completely different take and different slant on life I certainly never had. I've seen my daughter Jasmine take on life in confident and adventuresome ways that I'd never have been able to do at her age. In fact, I still struggle to do as well as she does in my 40s. She grasped the concepts of maturity and responsibility long before I ever did and from what I have seen, this is quite typical with older homeschoolers.

I have observed incredible diversity in these homeschooled young adults and appreciated their surprisingly mature points of view on issues. I have marveled at how many activities, goals and dreams they manage to fit into their lives that I, as a public schooled child, ever dreamed of having the opportunity to even attempt. I often find myself envying them their accomplishments—their traveling, their fledgling businesses, their open minded attitudes that resulted in breaking down so many of the barriers I remember from high school. I see a wonderful absence of cliques with these kids; the primitive divisions that are often painfully clear in high school are blurry here. Certainly some homeschooling kids tend to band together, but it is usually based on similar interests, not on income, clothing brands, grades or ages as it commonly is in public school. Here 21 year-olds think nothing of hanging out with 17 year-olds; 17 year-olds think nothing about being with 15 year-olds. Age or grade level loses its importance in the homeschooling teen world and it allows them the chance to learn from each other.

Where Do We Go From Here?

Homeschooling a teen isn't always easy—parenting a teenager in any respect usually isn't easy. There have certainly been moments with my own teenage daughter that I felt intensely frustrated at how to be the best parent I could—and manage to keep my sanity (and temper) at the same time. I struggled with everything from what to say when she wanted to get her nose pierced (inwardly screaming NOOOOOO!!!) to standing in the bathroom and actually helping her dye her waist-long, gorgeous corn silk blonde hair (gulp) purple. There are still moments now when I'm sure she is thinking that her father and I are not two of the brightest people she knows, but I suspect our intelligence level will increase with age—her age, that is. However, I also recognize these years can also be the most delightful, the most exciting and the most profound and I watch my child transitioning into an adult and while I might do things differently (what parent wouldn't?), I respect her unique path and watch her with love and pride.

A last note on a personal experience that recently brought home an important point to me about the perspective of some people out there in the "real world." While being interviewed by a journalist for an article in an Indiana newspaper, I was asked the typical question of whether or not my oldest daughter was going to go to college. I said, no, I didn't believe that she was, at least not at this point in her life. His response stunned me—even though by now, I suppose it shouldn't have. He asked me, in complete seriousness: "Then how will she ever be successful?" I paused, balancing my initial emotional reactions with the knowledge that I was also being quoted for the public to read and replied as follows: "Obviously your definition of success and mine differ quite a bit, as mine doesn't require a college degree. My def-

After Homeschool
Fifteen Homeschoolers Out In The Real World

Chapter One

inition of a successful life is one in which you are happy, healthy, you love and are loved in return, and you're doing something fulfilling and meaningful with your time. If my children have those things, they will be wondrously successful and I will have done the best possible job as a parent." I could wish for little more, for all four of my children, than these achievements.

This conversation has come back to me again and again during the writing of this book. If a person's qualification for whether or not the young adults in this book, or any other homeschoolers he/she meets are truly successful, is going to college, then the reader may well be sorely disappointed. Each young adult in this book is tremendously successful—they are living it, breathing it, exploring it and immersing themselves in it. For some going to a university plays a role in this success, but for others, it doesn't. While a college degree may be one of the many factors in a person's eventual success, these young people are proof that it certainly is not a requirement.

As children emerge from the world of childhood into young adulthood, the hours that we, as parents, spent teaching, loving and nurturing them begins to show. It's one of the miracles of parenthood to watch your children blossom and grow in unexpected ways. With homeschooling, this is especially true. It's a fascinating journey for all involved. So sit back and read the profiles of fifteen homeschoolers who have packed their bags and are ready to depart on their very unique journeys to adulthood. This book will give you a precious glimpse into a brand new and very unique generation of young people and the incredible variety of ways they are beginning to live their lives.

Tamra Orr
Portland, OR
April 24, 2003

Chapter Two

Gwen—Hear Me Roar!

Talking to Gwen is like talking to someone who has managed to gain a great deal of wisdom in a mere 22 years. She is confident, articulate—and knows just what she wants from her life—something people twice her age often wish for. Gwen has had the unique opportunity to spend time in public school, private school and home school and the experiences she gained at all three places helped to create this rather profound young woman.

When Gwen's mother, Olga, first decided to homeschool her children, her first child, Alexander, was already in preschool. "Homeschooling wasn't in my universe in the 1970s," she says. "It wasn't on anyone's radar screen yet." However, one incident sent her on the search for alternatives. "My son's class was told to draw a picture of their pets," she explains. "Alex drew a picture of his much loved pet chameleon, Jack, and in the picture, he resembled a dinosaur more than a lizard. The teacher held it up in front of the class, said this wasn't a pet and that Alex should only draw a dog or cat. He was so upset. I almost tore my hair out!"

Chapter Two

Luckily for the family, Olga happened to catch a television interview with John Holt soon after that episode. "I began talking to homeschoolers and discovered they didn't have the same mind-set on education," says Olga. A few months later, while standing in line to vote, Olga struck up a conversation with the woman in front of her—who turned out to be homeschooling her children. "It was like a sign from God and I accosted her after we voted," adds Olga. Soon, Alex was out of preschool and infant Gwen was company for her brother. Back then, it was necessary for Olga to have state permission to homeschool and so she got an attorney to help her. "I was able to register as a private school," she explains, "and I had the three first floor exits they required! We never really did school at home though; I just set textbooks and curriculum around as decoys. " When Alexander came home for Christmas vacation that year, he just didn't go back.

It wasn't easy, however. While homeschooling is quite accepted by much of society today, 15-plus years ago, it was either completely unheard of or looked down upon. "I would go places with Alexander and literally be attacked by people," says Olga. "I seemed to be the target of every little old lady who wanted to know why my child was not in school and would get disapproving looks and to have everyone you know and don't know against you is tough."

Fortunately, Olga's husband was quite supportive of her new educational decision. "He had complete faith in what I could do," she says. Unfortunately, her husband also passed away a few years later and homeschooling had to take a new turn. "I was home-schooled until the first grade," says Gwen. "When my dad died,

Hear Me Roar!

I began attending private school and remember the class fairly well," she adds. "I enjoyed being with the kids but felt like I could never please my teacher. I was reading at high school level then, but wasn't too big on math. All she ever did was say something negative to me about it." When the family had to move away from their farm the following year, Gwen entered a public school where most of the students' families were quite affluent. She was there for two years, then the family moved back to the farm and Gwen had her first real negative school experience. "I absolutely hated the public school—it was horrible and the kids were nasty. Mom pulled me out and homeschooled me for the rest of 4th grade. I preferred it because there weren't any mean spirited kids around to make me cry," admits Gwen. For the next two years (5th and 6th grades), Gwen was back in private school but she grew bored and restless and by the time junior high rolled around, Olga had made the decision to just let her stay home again. She would stay there until she took community college classes at 16 and then went on to college.

How were the teen years for Gwen? The usual fears that parents homeschooling older children have began to filter in. "When she hit 13, I started feeling a little nervous," says Olga. "I began to worry that she would need to know stuff that I didn't know and so I enrolled in her a correspondence school."

Gwen remembers this clearly. "Mom was starting to freak out about things, so I enrolled in this course at 14," she recalls, "to try to get some 'higher education', but that didn't work out very well. It was really boring and I wasn't learning so I quit. Instead, I spent a LOT of time at the library. The Dewey Decimal system and card catalogs became my best friends," she says with a smile.

After Homeschool
Fifteen Homeschoolers Out In The Real World

Chapter Two

"I was wrong to enroll Gwen in that program," reflects Olga. "I wish I had kept to a looser approach. In my opinion, there is no such thing as an experience that couldn't be educational. We were always immersed in educational things, from doing fractions in the kitchen to geometry at the museum or on the table at Burgerville."

While Gwen was making some of her educational choices, she was also leading a rather whirlwind life socially—debunking the myth that homeschoolers have problems with socialization. "While I was growing up," she says, "I had more extra-curricular activities than any other kid I knew. I did gymnastics, which was my all time favorite. I became competitive and even made it to nationals before I quit. I went horseback riding, swimming and junior life-guarding. I was in Girl Scouts, where I was president of my troop and received the second highest award possible, and I took baton, ballet, tap, jazz and when I was ten, I went to cheerleading camp. Basically," she continues, "I was allowed to do anything that I showed interest in. How my mom was able to take me to all of these different activities, plus my sibling's, while managing to be a single mother who owned her own business, I have no idea!"

In addition to all of these activities, Gwen also went to three homecoming dances and was crowned Miss Junior America Newberg, where she rode on the back of a red convertible in a parade. "I was also in the Miss America Co-Ed Preteen competition," adds Gwen. "But since I didn't smile during the talent portion, they gave me second place."

Hear Me Roar!

"Public schools just have the wrong kind of socialization," adds Olga. "Children can have much healthier interactions outside of school. I feel that public schools are hotbeds of everything awful and I cannot see how kids can learn there."

At age 16, Gwen began taking courses at the local community college, including writing, French and as much dance as possible. At 18, she moved out of her mom's house and into her own place. "I was going full time to the community college and working a full time job at a day care center," she explains. "I left the house at eight in the morning and didn't come home until after ten." It was too much and a year later, Gwen dropped out of college. "I picked becoming an adult over getting a higher education," she says. "I wanted some kind of social life. That's one thing homeschooling does for some people; it makes you really dislike the regular classroom setting. You miss being able to roam around, look at things and explore, rather than having to sit in a hard chair listening to a burned out professor drone on for two hours."

In her quest to become an adult, Gwen found a job at a local bookstore—one of the biggest bookstores in the country. "I started at the cash register," she says. "Then I applied to take over the mystery section of the store and got it. I was put in the children's room too because of my day care experience. Soon after," she continues, "I assisted in the sidelines department (bookmarks, stationary, etc.) and now I am a buyer for the company." At 22, Gwen is responsible for over $60,000 of purchasing power, and has

Chapter Two

recently been promoted to be the liaison with the local schools. "I love my job!" she says with a big smile. "I am very fast and know that I can do anything that I put my mind to because my mom taught me *how* to think and learn, not what to!"

Along with a job she loves, there is a person also. "Spencer is a whole lot of wonderful," says Gwen with a twinkle in her eye. The couple has been together for three and a half years and became engaged in October of 2002. "We met through friends," explains Gwen, "and when I saw him, my jaw hit the floor." The wedding is set for 2004. "I picture her marrying Spencer, having children and living happily ever after," says Olga. "She will have whatever future she chooses."

Olga speaks of the role her religion had in her homeschooling. "Faith is very important to me," she explains. "I am definitely a committed Christian and I used Bible books and tapes in our homeschooling but I used other curricula too. I figured that I raised my children with strong enough faith to not be shaken."

To Olga, the greatest benefit of homeschooling her children is simple: time. "The best thing for me was being able to spend so much time with them and make sure they received the best possible education they could. School is so ridiculously time consuming and it was wonderful to have the freedom to have fun together and do things. I thoroughly enjoyed homeschooling all of my kids and wish I could keep doing it," she adds. Alexander is now 27 and a "computer geek for Intel", while Gwen's younger sister, Natalia or Talli, is 19 and started her community college classes at 14.

Hear Me Roar!

Gwen looks back at her education and puts it this way. "I think I'm a lot more pleasant to be around than if I had gone to public school. I will be first to admit, I am a people pleaser. I would've gone crazy trying to please eight teachers. I also think I've been able to realize my intelligence a lot more fully than I would have in a classroom setting. I realized the educational benefits of not being stuck in a classroom with 30 other kids, not to mention if I went faster that I was 'supposed to', I would get praised instead of scolded. My mom taught me how to think so I could come up with answers to questions by myself instead of (a) being in the dark and just never learning or (b) having everything spoon fed for me. I wish that I hadn't done any regular school because I think I would be better off now if I hadn't. By the same token," she adds. "perhaps I wouldn't appreciate my homeschooling background as much if I didn't experience the horror that is the public school system."

"When I was an adolescent," she continues, "I had a lot of friends who asked me why I liked homeschooling. Didn't I miss the other kids, didn't I want to go to dances and football games and all that other high school stuff. I told them I'd gone to three homecomings (and by the way, they suck) and I find that sitting out in the hard bleachers in the freezing cold, cheering on a team

Chapter Two

that I don't know or care anything about, doesn't strike me as being even remotely entertaining, much less something I would give up a perfectly good Saturday night to endure! I prefer to sit in my cozy house," she adds, "and read a good book. If that book happens to be the *Atlas of the Human Anatomy, Billions and Billions* or the complete works of William Shakespeare, so be it. I am homeschooler; hear me roar!"

Chapter Three

Daniel—The Moral Divide

While the United States has made great progress in not only making homeschooling legal in all fifty states, but relaxing some of the restrictions put upon it, other countries are not quite as advanced. Daniel, 18, and his family have found this out the hard way; as part of a US military family, they are currently stationed in Germany where homeschooling is illegal. "There are many Americans in the area," says his mother Cindy, "and we have no real relationship with the Germans. I'm not sure if it is because the Germans are just not gregarious people by nature or if it is because we are Americans." Scheduled to leave in spring of 2003, Daniel adds, "Since we are US military, we can play by the US rules for homeschooling. There

Chapter Three

is a support group here for American homeschoolers but most of the kids are a lot younger so we aren't involved." Daniel's siblings include two grown sisters, as well as a younger brother named Timothy.

Both of the girls attended Christian schools in the beginning, but then homeschooled for five years, before going on to Christian colleges. Currently, one is a mathematician with the National Security Agency, while the other is a registered nurse at Washington DC's National Children's Medical Center.

Timothy and Daniel, on the other hand, were homeschooled from kindergarten on except for two years in an elementary Christian school. What caused the shift from Christian schools to home? "My husband and I were quite disappointed in the only local Christian school because they seemed to be simply teaching the tests instead of helping our children actually learn," says Cindy. "We felt the public school's curriculum was at odds with our faith. We wanted more control over the things our children would be taught. We also were interested in shielding one of our young children from the unkind behavior we often observed in most school settings. Over time," she adds, "shielding became less of a concern. Flexibility was also a great benefit as we have moved six times since we began homeschooling, including two trips to Europe." This military family has seen quite a bit of the world in their years together, including Florida, Illinois, Tennessee, Washington DC and Texas, plus England and Germany. Some stays were as short as six months, while others have lasted four years. "I wish we could have taken better advantage of some of the

The Moral Divide

places we've lived in educating our children," says Cindy. "I believe it would have broadened their understanding of many things. However, the children quickly learned from all of the moving that family is what you've got—we are the ones who are here forever."

Daniel appreciates the shielding his parents provided. "I think the greatest benefit of homeschooling is the sheltering we so often hear about from home schooling detractors," he says. "For about the first 13 years of my life, my parents were able to shape my personality and values. With no competing viewpoints to choose from, my parents were able to help me build a foundation of values that will stay with me for the rest of my life. I also developed a strong relationship with them," he adds. "Many non-homeschoolers have neither the firm moral grounding nor the close relationship with their parents that I have enjoyed. They don't have it because they live their lives in the midst of competing viewpoints; I have it because I was protected from those things that would harm me at an early age. Now I am able to handle those situations and my parents are willing to draw back the shelter."

Joe and Cindy's initial decision to homeschool was supported not only by an excellent support group but, then, a parent could call experts Dorothy and Raymond Moore on the phone and ask them any question. They also referred to the Moore's books, as well as Mary Pride's. Initially, the family chose a curriculum requiring a high level of creativity and instruction on the part of the teacher—but quickly found this to be far too demanding. "In the beginning, we had a lot of fouls when it came to what

Chapter Three

curricula to use," says Cindy. "What worked for me didn't always work for each child. It's hard to select the right curriculum for each child to achieve appropriate educational goals without putting too much burden on teacher or child." Now the family uses a curriculum that is self-teaching. Daniel likes this approach better.

"Because we are in Germany now, I needed a more Internet based curricula," he explains. "We're enrolled in the Alpha Omega Academy Online. It's an excellent option because it is so user-friendly and now I'm using a computer-based, self-instructional curriculum," he explains. "The publishers have teachers available to help me if I have difficulty with a concept. The Academy also has a Virtual Campus on the Internet that allows students to get to know each other through chat rooms and bulletin boards." Daniel's mother is pleased about this program too. "I don't have to know calculus for my children to take calculus," she says.

Daniel has spent some time doing volunteer work, as many older homeschoolers do. "When I was in 9th and 10th grade, I started working as a Red Cross volunteer at the Security Forces building on Scott Air Force Base," he says. "I helped the Air Force police in the Pass and Registration office. I was there for two years and I was good enough that I really became a part of the team." The time spent volunteering helped with what Daniel refers to as "typical teenage antsyness. It was a nice release for me," he adds. "It made me feel like I was doing something with real world impact; an opportunity to make a difference and help people. I

The Moral Divide

couldn't say that for any of the schoolwork I was doing." In Germany, Daniel also worked as an office assistant in one of the Air Force offices. "My first few days there, I shredded documents and washed windows," he says. "By the time I left, I had hung over 35 pictures, created spread-sheets and given a briefing to a board of officers."

One of the biggest parts of Daniel's life is JROTC, a program run by the Air Force that is very similar to the older ROTC program, including uniforms, marching, saluting and drills. "Its technical motto is to build better citizens," says Daniel. "It focuses on leadership training as in character development plus aerospace education. This year I am the Group Public Affairs Officer. " As the only homeschooler in his JROTC class, set in the public high school, he sometimes feels out of place. "Many of the projects and activities they design are based on the public school environment," says Daniel, "and I have to keep reminding them that I am homeschooled. They get this strange look on their faces that say they think I'm weird, but okay." Daniel is editor of his JROTC newsletter, writing articles, doing interviews and teaching other cadets how to write a decent newspaper piece. He hopes to go into sports journalism in college. "I enjoy writing," he says, "and would like to be a sports announcer someday—particularly in baseball and football." The JROTC plays a heavy role in Daniel's future as well. His dedication and hard work have certainly paid off. He was recently accepted at Union University, a private

Chapter Three

Christian school, with a full four-year tuition scholarship from the Air Force ROTC and was awarded a congressional nomination to the Air Force Academy by both Congressman Charles Gonzalez (D-TX) and Senator John Cornyn (R-TX). On the other hand, younger brother Timothy "goes to the beat of a different drummer," according to Cindy. "Daniel and I have the same beliefs," he says, "but we have different career choices; different plans for our futures. He plans to be in the Air Force—I plan to write comic books and form a rock band!" Despite their differences, the boys stay close. "There is no 'get away little brother' attitude here," says Cindy. "They are very different people with different personalities, but they still can stay up talking together late at night."

Daniel's parents hope several things for their children in the future. "It's tough to know the future," says Cindy with a chuckle. "I suspect all four of our children will marry and begin raising a family in a Christian home. I pray they will be men and women after God's own heart and will impact the world for Christ."

Religious faith is an integral part of Daniel's family and education and occasionally, it has created a rift between him and his peers. "Our boys have been confronted with a moral divide between them and their church youth group peers who attend public school," says Cindy. "This divide has made it difficult for them to relate to kids their age because our boys' standards are generally much higher than those of their friends." Daniel agrees this has been an occasional problem—but in learning how to cope

The Moral Divide

with it, has learned some priceless life lessons. "I am still working on how to deal with people who have opposite viewpoints from mine. When I saw my peers who didn't have the same values, I had difficulty. My natural reaction was to inform them their actions were very wrong. I found out that it was not a great way to win friends and influence people—plus they weren't listening to me anyway," he admits with a chuckle. "Instead I try to lead by example and ask myself, 'Can I address an issue with a form of love?' If not, I back off. It's an ignorant viewpoint to suggest that anyone has to hold the same beliefs as the people they know in order to have a cordial working relationship. A person can tolerate a lot of viewpoints without having to understand them. I had adjusted my attitudes towards people, treating them with more love than judgment," adds Daniel. "That is a skill that will improve with time and practice."

When Daniel graduates in 2003, Joe and Cindy aren't sure how it will be celebrated. "There isn't much interest among the few graduating homeschoolers in Germany in a commencement ceremony," says Cindy. "But we will do something. Even if it's on a small scale. Daniel keeps telling us that he will just whistle 'Pomp and Circumstance' as he walks through the living room," she adds with a smile.

Chapter Three

Looking back on his education, Daniel says that he feels it was far superior to anything he could have gotten in public school and advises other parents to start homeschooling as early as possible. "Start before they turn 13," he says. "If you have them learning in the home at an early age, they will get used to the idea that school is done at home. The earlier you start, the easier it will be." Cindy's comments are simple. "The only way to save this generation is to homeschool them. High school is the gateway to the future for most children, so parents and students may be tempted to overstress about it. Don't make it too hard on yourselves. Do your best and trust God."

Chapter Four

Laurie—An Unprocessed Child

When 22 year-old Laurie looks back at her homeschooling education, she is amazingly aware at some of the distinct advantages she had. Unlike some situations, she had an extended network playing part in her education. "My 'instruction' came in tidbits from friends and relatives. Sometimes it came unsolicited, like a visit from an evangelist," she says laughingly "Uncle Jim taught me how to write my

Chapter Four

name in cursive; Mawmaw taught me how to add large numbers; Aunt Laura showed me the basics of algebra and a neighbor named Lynn critiqued my poetry and helped improve my writing. I learned reading from people reading to me. I learned everything else myself by living. I learned cooking, theory, fractions, sewing, making crafts, animal care and other things just by hanging around the house." However, ask Laurie if she was missing anything in her education and she will reply, "Yes—a lack of a supportive community!"

At the time her family began their journey into homeschooling, there was a serious lack of encouragement for the unschooling style they had chosen. "Mom was the only one I knew throughout my entire childhood and most of my teenhood who believed that I could learn naturally," she explains. "Even my dad was uncertain. I had no unschooling peers or role models and I lived in an ultra-conservative cultural backwater in southwest Louisiana. I think I would've felt more secure with myself if I had had the advantage of a supportive community," she adds. Homeschooling without adequate support from family or community is always more challenging. "We knew some homeschoolers from a local support group, but we just weren't on the same page as they were," says Laurie. "The only reasons they seemed to want to homeschool were that public schools didn't use enough punishment or teach enough Bible."

Laurie's mother, Valerie, knew she wanted to homeschool her daughter before she was even born. (Laurie is an only child.) "I found school to be an absolute waste of time," she says with a distinctive southern drawl. "When I was pregnant, my sister-in-law gave me a copy of *Summerhill: A Radical Approach to Child-Rearing* by A.S. Neill. I knew after reading it, I would not raise any children in the traditional authoritative ways, nor would they attend school unless they asked to attend," she continues. "I came to believe in unschooling because I believed in what Neill, John Holt and others said about a child's innate ability to learn and the harm in forced learning. I had no idea what impact their words would have on our lives. Twenty two years later, I am more convinced than ever that unschooling is the ONLY decent way to raise a child."

An Unprocessed Child

While Laurie agrees with her mother's choice in homeschooling methods, she does have one complaint. "I wish that my mom had fully explained to me why she choose to unschool much earlier than she did. This would have given me more confidence. As it was, Mom took for granted that I knew why we were unschooling just because we were unschooling. I needed more assurance that I wasn't going to turn out to be a basket case like others predicted. "Actual understanding of her mother's decision came when Laurie herself read Neill's Summerhill book. "It enlightened me," she says, "and I wish I had read it much, much earlier."

Valerie remembers well the way her family originally reacted to her decision to homeschool Laurie. "I got some flack," she recalls. Valerie had already made some unconventional parenting choices, including vegetarianism. "My family knew I was intelligent but homeschooling was just one more step. My sister is a public school teacher, and although we are very close friends now, we are definitely on opposite sides of the fence when it comes to education. As for my parents," she continues, "they didn't criticize but they didn't approve either." Along with not approving, they didn't ask questions or try to understand what their daughter was doing. "We were interviewed for the local paper," explains Valerie with an infectious laugh, "and my mom's friends, who live a hundred miles away, saw it. They were just raving about the article and she was absolutely clueless. So, now she is proud of us but supportive—nah!" Valerie's in-laws, on the other hand, are literally in awe of her homeschooling. "They think I am some kind of goddess," she chuckles.

Laurie has never wanted to go to school and says when she was young, she remembers feeling sorry for the neighborhood children who lined up to get on the school bus in the mornings. 'I felt like I was extremely lucky to have parents that were cool enough to let me stay home." That attitude did have a few ups and downs, of course. "I went through a crisis period when I was about 16," says Laurie. "I knew I was getting close to adulthood and didn't know what to do about it. I didn't know what the future held; I was insecure and wondered if I would be on track or have a better plan if I was in public school. I had

Chapter Four

no math skills because I had always passionately resisted any of my parents' attempts to show me how to multiply and divide and I punished myself psychologically for not knowing these things when people half my age knew them. I remember crying and asking Mom why she hadn't forced me to learn math even though I didn't want to. She told me that she had always had confidence that I would learn whatever I needed when I needed it."

It turned out that Laurie's mom was right. "First, I tried taking some high school adult math classes," says Laurie. "I sat at a table in the cafeteria and studied the text and asked questions and it was pointless. Just horrible. I quit and went through a brief period of despair. However, when I got to college," Laurie continues, "I found out that I was very receptive to math in an adult, non mandatory classroom setting and I went from remedial math to senior level statistics with straight A's. My story had a happy ending," she says with the same contagious laugh as her mother. Valerie remembers those days also. "Laurie was a bit hard on herself for her lack of math skills," she says. "Remembering my own feelings of angst during those years made it much easier to empathize with her and continue giving her the respect and patience that she needed." Now, looking back on this time of her life, Laurie says, "What was my 'math crisis' compared to being force-fed knowledge in school or strict home-schooling and coming to hate it? I have friends who are just as smart as I am but turned away from learning for the sake of learning because school damaged their sensibilities so much. I don't know if that would have happened to me, but I am glad my parents didn't take that chance!"

During her teen years, Laurie did some volunteer work, including participation in a church-affiliated outreach program that provided food and clothes for the poor, as well as selling some things and staffing a cooperative craft store. "I periodically fed the neighbors' animals and watered their plants while they were on vacation," says Laurie, "I got my first 'real' job at a video store when I was 18." That job was to lead her to a turning point in her life. "When Laurie started to feel as if she had no future goals," says Valerie, "I suggested that she get a job." Laurie followed that advice. "Getting a job is important," says Laurie. "It is what made me want to go on to school. I want-

An Unprocessed Child

ed to do something more cerebral." Valerie remembers the exact incident that triggered her daughter's desire to go on to college. "One night while she was working in that video store," she recalls, "she saw the manager counting the receipts and closing the store for the day. She said to me, 'I know I don't want to be doing this kind of job when I am in my 40s,'" adds Valerie. "The next day she got a college catalog and practically memorized it. That minimum wage job helped her to decide. She saw no joy in working for others and receiving such low pay for her efforts."

Laurie went to college at 18 and graduated with a BA in Sociology in less than four years. She had a 3.98 GPA and as Valerie says, "I envy her insatiable thirst for knowledge." In fact, she envied it enough that she actually started college with her. "We registered at the same time," she says.

Currently, Laurie is working two different jobs, one in a law office and one in a bookstore. She is also preparing to go back to her local college for pre-med studies, then on to medical school. "I want to be some sort of doctor," she says. "I want to do something meaningful." Valerie pictures a wonderful future for her child also. "I picture Laurie as a happy adult who will know what she wants and go after it. She will do whatever she enjoys."

Valerie's enrollment in college led her to her biggest project, next to her daughter. "I wrote an essay on unschooling for my English class," she explains, "and my teacher encouraged me to put my thoughts and ideas into a book. The seed was planted and it grew for two years. In the beginning, it was just about unschooling but I couldn't separate parenting and education and so I ended up with more than fifty topics from chores to dating to daily life, each one with examples from Laurie's childhood." Valerie headed to a remote cabin in Canada for several weeks and wrote quickly on the computer there. "The first draft was done in two weeks," says Laurie. "My mom just immersed herself in it. I was the editor for the book." The result was the new book *The Unprocessed Child: Living Without School* published by Unbounded Publications (www.geocities.com/theunprocessedchild.)

After Homeschool
Fifteen Homeschoolers Out In The Real World

Chapter Four

Other books on Valerie's recommended reading list include Mary Griffith's *Unschooling Handbook*, Howard Gardner's *Unschooled Mind*, Carl Rogers' *Freedom to Learn*, John Taylor Gatto's *Dumbing Us Down*, Ivan Illich's *Deschooling Society* and Joseph Chilton Pearce's *Magical Child*. Both mother and daughter also recommend the teenager homeschooling classic *Teenage Liberation Handbook* by Grace Llewellyn (who wrote the Foreword to this book). "Get a copy of TLH because it is amazing," says Laurie. She also has some advice for parents. "Stop being a parent and be a friend," she says. "Don't judge—listen. I think that all teenagers need is an adult who remembers what it was like and is able to do some active listening and sympathizing. Respect your teen's feelings and opinions and support any academic or career ambitions. Know that 18 is not a magical age to graduate and start being an adult. Your child can be ready for 'grown up' responsibilities at 16 or 25. Lastly, know that college is wonderful for some, but necessary for none."

Laurie and Valerie both look back on their homeschooling years as a fabulous experience. "It was all easy and all the best," says Valerie. "I can honestly say that I never had a doubt about unschooling or felt uneasy in the least. Being Laurie's mother," she adds, "has been wonderful for every minute of the 22 years." Laurie says much the same. "How has unschooling changed my life compared to how it might have been in public school? That's the million-dollar question, isn't it? Who knows what would have happened if I had spent 12 years serving a mandatory prison . . . eh, school sentence? I have sometimes wished that I could've cloned myself and put the clone in school just to see how I would have turned out, but I decided that I could never do that because I couldn't, even hypothetically, be instrumental in putting anyone in school!"

Essay

Voice of an Autodidact

by Lindsey Johnson

(reprinted with permission from the author and from Home Education Magazine, May/June 1998 issue)

Some things make me wonder what this country is striving for—one of those things is school. I do not understand why we would want to take children away from their families and force them to learn and to learn our way. I do not understand why we would want to separate information into "subjects", tearing away all the connectedness of knowledge and teaching that everything is unrelated, something that is (obviously, I hope) untrue; to create abstract tests that in no way accurately measure intellect, or to give grades for something (learning) that should be as breathing and separate from life; to segregate ages, etc., implying that learning must be done away from all unless they are like you... that you cannot learn anything from someone younger or older than you, nor can you learn something from someone who may know more or less about something than you do (and vice versa). Things like these (and there are many, many more), make me wonder about school.

Voice of an Autodidact

I have been unschooled my entire life, my only brushes with school being in preschool and in driver's ed last summer. I've basically learned whatever has befallen my curiosity and wonder... my parents have pretty much allowed me the freedom to choose. Only recently, though, have I become completely comfortable with this.

When I was younger, I pretty much learned whatever my heart desired, from building with Legos®, sometimes with instructions and sometimes without, to reading a book a day, to writing to 40-60 pen pals, to publishing my own pen pal newsletter. Looking back now, I realize that I did learn a lot, almost always self-taught (except for when I asked my parents for help or found what I needed from books or other sources). But I always said that I'd go to school someday. My parents always said it was my choice.

Last year, I thought I'd like some structure, so I enrolled in a correspondence course. Now, my experience may not mirror that of another, but I really didn't like it. It was OK at first, but then I started seeing the senselessness of it and the fact that I was using boring textbooks and taking tests that, even though I wasn't in school, controlled my mind. I had a stack of books to read that I didn't read because I was reading textbooks and didn't have any energy left over to read a real book.

Then I read Grace Llewellyn's *Teenage Liberation Handbook* (see Foreword), which pretty much changed my life. It made me realize that I don't need a requirement to tell me what I should learn or should have learned by now and I don't need a textbook or a test to show me I learned or did not learn something. I don't need a grade to tell me if what I learned was satisfactorily learned and I can take control of my own life and path. I'm sorry I lost that time I spend in the correspondence school, which I could have used to do important things but I am glad that I figured out, through not actually having to go, that school is not a place I enjoy.

I've been around school people a lot. I've had people tell me that I should go to school or I wouldn't know anything or be anything; then I wouldn't say much. Knowing what I know now, though, I'd love to get into a nice debate with them. I'm not so

After Homeschool
Fifteen Homeschoolers Out In The Real World

by Lindsey Johnson

silly to think they would automatically change their views, but I do believe they might rethink them. I think many people's opposition to homeschooling stems from ignorance. Most people are just dead set against the freedom to learn on your own and to choose what you learn and if you'll have someone to help you.

I believe there is a beauty in learning, rather, in the learning you initiate, instead of something you do to satisfy a requirement. The beauty is lost when learning is required and it becomes an arduous race to the finish when it should be a great journey. What is learned should be the choice of the learner. When learning happens this way, not only is it more effective but its beauty is more apparent and more truthful. In compulsory schooling there is no beauty, for it is required. There is no heart in it, as there can hardly be heart in something that is compulsory. Would volunteering be as rewarding if it were required or every citizen? No, because no one would be in it for the joy; they would only be satisfying a requirement. It's the same with learning; when learning is required, it is no longer beautiful, it is no longer spirited, it is no longer meaningful. Requirement deadens it.

I've often thought about this while I am hiking in the woods or browsing through the bookstore on a wintry day. Why would I want to trade this in for a classroom? Why had I ever thought that I would want to? In our lovely, pro-school society, some people would tell me that I could learn better if I traded in the earth or beautiful words for a stifling, spiritless classroom that controlled me. I wish they could see that this is not true.

I do find it disheartening that some people, when they are told how we unschool and that our learning is self-directed, say, "Well, that's great for you but I could never do it" or "My children aren't that self-motivated; they don't have any interests."

First of all, you can do it. Somehow, anything can be done. To live meaningfully is something anyone can do, all it takes is desire and an open mind and heart. Secondly, how do you know your children aren't that self-motivated when they haven't been able to follow their own beat and have always been told what,

Voice of an Autodidact

how and when to learn? How could anyone be self-motivated under those terms? The thing I have come to love most about unschooling is that I get to follow my own beat. We've never had school-at-home and that is wonderful. What I have learned I have never thought of as school work (except for the correspondence course). It is funny how some interests go in spurts. When I was younger, I loved to read and I wrote little stories and poems. Then, there were a few years where I hardly wrote or read at all. I used that time to do other things.

What I am saying is how boring life would be if we learned basically the same things every year. History I, History II, History III and so on. That is incredibly boring and meaningless. Everything is interconnected and it isn't necessary to separate information. When this is done, all the whole interconnectedness of knowledge and information is broken. When information is fragmented into subjects and presented in pieces, it is not whole; it is broken. Doesn't that make knowledge seem limited? This world is whole. According to school, it is broken into pieces and must be learned about through fragmentation and ringing bells. That, I feel, is sad.

My mind has opened up tremendously this past year. Not only have I started doing the things I love and are important to me, but I do not question myself as much as I used to if my ideas do not correspond with the popular ideas. I have begun to realize that the world is interconnected and that learning is fun and wonderful. I have become stronger in my convictions and happier with my choices.

After Homeschool
Fifteen Homeschoolers Out In The Real World

by Lindsey Johnson

And it's funny—when I started doing what I enjoyed and learning what I love through living, everything started to happen. I suppose that only when one realizes that the only way to learn is through living does one truly start to live. I often wonder why I never went to school as I thought I would so many times. The only explanation that I can think of is that I knew all along that unschooling was what I wanted, that I didn't want to go to school; it just took me awhile to uncover what I knew in my heart to be true. Things seem so much clearer and I am so much happier.

Now that I realize my freedom, I'm quite protective of it. At this point, I am pretty sure that my life and learning will venture away from college, partly because my career choices don't require a degree; partly because I do not see the purpose for me to go; partly because, as I value my freedom, I am wary of giving it up to a university. Right now, I don't see how college could benefit me. I shall let the whole world by my Harvard and my Yale.

I am so glad my parents made the initial choice to unschool me. I do sometimes wish that I could have discovered earlier how lucky I am but I'm also glad that I found out when I did. I can now proudly say that I am an autodidact. Unschooling has become my choice now but I would have been able to make my choice had my parents not first "rebelled" and made theirs.

Voice of an Autodidact

(Postscript: A word from Lindsey: "This was written when I was 16, nearly 5 years ago. It expressed many of my views at the time. Some of it I would write again, some I would not. It was true when it was written, though. I currently live in Georgia and now go to college after taking two 'gap years' in which I traveled to Israel and Egypt, and volunteered for the Salt Lake City 2002 Olympic Torch Relay, among other things. I'm moving to California next year and plan to major in anthropology, although I'm not exactly sure where that's going to take me. Anyway, in unschooler fashion, I'm following it for now. We shall see.")

Chapter Five

Ben—A Sincere Prayer

Listening to Benjamin talk about his past is both difficult and inspiring. He has seen the darker side of life and almost gave into it and then, he found an answer that he believes saved him in several ways.

Homeschooled since the third grade, Benjamin is now 20 years old and living a life that he finds both fulfilling and full of possibilities. However, he had to work hard to get to that point and his story touches onto a lot of the issues young people face today.

When Benjamin's parents decided to homeschool him, as well as his four younger siblings, it was a decision primarily based on their Christian faith and the lack of it in their own educational backgrounds. "I grew up mostly in public schools, being taught a secular world view," says Benjamin's father. "When I was saved,

Chapter Five

I began to develop a more Biblical world view. I wanted my children to have this benefit through schooling; more of an integrated world view." Benjamin's mother agrees. "I grew up in a non-Christian home. My dad was gone a lot and being the youngest of seven, I felt like my mom just didn't seem to have a great interest in being very involved with my life. I attended public schools," she adds, "and pretty much felt alone in my home and at school. I wanted my children to have maximum parental involvement in their home life and school life." Both parents put a high priority on providing a Christian curriculum for their children and they used a variety of supplies from Christian Liberty Academy Satellite Schools. Over the course of their homeschooling years, they began creating their own curricula using several different sources. Benjamin's parents wanted to protect their children from the public school's worldly influences. In addition, they just wanted a better education than they felt a public school could provide.

Benjamin's initial reaction to being homeschooled was, "Cool! I get to stay home and sleep in and do whatever!'" he admits. "At the same time, I knew that this would mean loss of social contact. I soon realized that to make new friends, I had to go around the block or build relationships with other kids I met through violin lessons or baseball." Benjamin was the first child in his family to be homeschooled and so, in several ways, he felt like a guinea pig. "I think that my parents did really well," he says, "but if I chose to homeschool my own kids, I'd make sure they got into sports, learned an instrument and got everything any other

A Sincere Prayer

normal kid would. My younger siblings have it made!" His parents basically agree. Their advice to other homeschoolers now is to get involved with a homeschool co-op, to utilize outside resources such as community colleges and to involve your kids in organized sports"

Benjamin did well at home until junior high. That is when some of his actual problems began. Benjamin explains it in a voice that is both strong and vulnerable. "At 14 years old, I began doing some rebellious things," he explains. "I hid things from my parents and got involved in pornography, not knowing what kind of trap it could be. I stopped living a Christian life." Benjamin had become a Christian at seven but, as he puts it, "It just went in one ear and out the other." This troubled stage of life lasted several years for Benjamin. "I had gone so far down the path by 17," he says, "that I was an expert at wearing a Christian mask and then going off to parties with friends." Soon, Benjamin found himself approaching a breaking point. "I wanted to be a self-sufficient person and yet, I couldn't run my life at all," he admits. Finally, he took a step that would change his life but had the potential to have ended it.

At 17, Benjamin attempted suicide. "I downed quite a bit of painkillers and then I just sat and cried for 30 minutes," he says. "My stomach began to burn and then I called my former girlfriend and told her what I had done." Benjamin's friend had the sense to call 911 and in a matter of minutes, Benjamin was on his way to the hospital in the back of an ambulance. Both of his par-

After Homeschool

Fifteen Homeschoolers Out In The Real World

Chapter Five

ents were away when all of this was happening, but just as the ambulance pulled away, his mother returned home to see fire trucks, police cars and an ambulance carry away her son.

At the hospital, Benjamin's stomach was pumped and he still calls it the worst experience of his entire life. Next, they took him to a mental hospital. "It was all trees and sunshine and smiley faces on the wall," he says sourly. "I was there for seven days and my family and I all had to go through counseling." After he was released, Benjamin was put on a prescription of anti-depressants but hated it. "It was a mind altering drug and after three days, I just quit taking it. I told my parents sometime later."

Benjamin found his solace and comfort in the very place his parents would have suggested in the first place—God. "I cried and prayed to God when I got home," he confesses, "and told Him that I had tried all I could do but nothing had worked, not even suicide. I didn't want to take the drugs and I just didn't know what else to do. I had tried so hard to be the 'good son' and set an example for my younger siblings." Benjamin says this was the most sincere prayer of his entire life and it actually resulted in a total turnaround for him and his entire family. "It was a real wake up call," he says. "I can now say that I am glad that it happened to me. It was like a cold shower."

Fortunately, Benjamin has a story with a happy ending. Since his turnaround, Benjamin has been keeping busy. He worked at a Christian Outdoor Adventure Camp for seven months and obtained some survival training as well as the chance to serve and teach others. He had several jobs including one at a large department store and one doing landscaping for a local company. Today

A Sincere Prayer

he is living in his own place and he works as an intern with a youth group and a pastor. He sets up worship teams and songs and helps to organize and plan events for the more than 150 kids in the group. Recently he also gave his first sermon in front of a camera. He will continue his internship for one year and hopes to go beyond that.

"I feel this job is helping me to grow in the spiritual gifts that God gave me," he says. His girlfriend is currently attending another college and when talking about her, he says with a smile, "We're pretty serious and heading to marriage. We'll wait until she graduates though so I will stick around for four more years." Benjamin is also considering getting an associate's degree from a local college and his parents are pleased with his life decisions so far. "While Ben has chosen not to attend college at this time," says his mother, "he has pursued other worthy experiences. I am proud of these choices and his endeavors."

For the long term, Benjamin hopes to go into the ministry as a youth pastor and leader of an outdoor camp. He is also toying with the idea of getting a real estate license as a 'financial back up plan,' he chuckles.

When he reflects back on his years of homeschooling, Benjamin still sees it as a positive experience. "The greatest benefit is that I could go at my own pace in every subject," he says. "I loved science, history and literature. With that passion, I was able to excel in those areas. On the flip side, I didn't like math and economics as much. Because my mom and dad were my teachers, I could sit down and work though the problems and not

Chapter Five

only finish the homework, but actually learn how the process is done. My education was an excellent one," he continues, "and I ended up getting my G.E.D. with such a high score, it was the equivalent to graduating high school with honors. I was able to graduate in my junior year."

What would have Benjamin's life been like if he had been in public school? "I think I would've been even more frustrated," he says. "I may have been more encouraged to get into alcohol, drugs and sex. With my background I know now what is right and wrong, but if I'd had a more secular environment and friends, I might have died of a drug overdose. It is pure speculation—I just don't know. I am more tight with my parents than I would've been if they had just sent me off to school. As I look back over it," he continues, "I wouldn't have it any other way. If you want a tight family, this is the way to go. In the teen years, I think that we tend to alienate ourselves from our families. We are becoming individuals, our own person. I had my rough times and did my rebellious things, but in the end, because of my parents who cared enough about me to educate me the way they did, we have a very tight family. I would have it no other way!"

Chapter Six

Initiative, Not Instruction

One of the first questions that older homeschoolers often are asked is, What about the prom? For some the answer is a simple, What about it? They have little or no interest in going and can't fathom what the big deal is about it. Others may respond with the fact that they have indeed gone to the prom with a date and their experiences ranged from dull and ridiculous to a great time. Still others just smile because they created their own prom. This was the case with Molly, 20. "I had been to high school proms before," she says, "but in my senior year, I wanted to create my own." With virtually no budget and a handful of other interested homeschoolers, it was a real grassroots effort. Built around the theme of William Shakespeare's *A Midsummer Night's Dream*, the homeschooling prom attracted almost one hundred people, some with and some without dates. The music was provided by a homeschooling D.J. and a King and Queen were elected, by a drawing and not by level of popularity. Girls wore formals and flowers— or whatever they felt like, including a couple who came regaled in complete dress and suit made out of duct tape.

Chapter Six

When it was over, there was a non-traditional after-prom party. Everyone slept outside in tents—boys in one, girls in another and lots of chaperones in between. "It was a wonderful success," says Susan, Molly's mother, "and it has continued on. Molly's younger sister Hannah helps in the planning." This homemade prom has been held for three years now and is still quite popular.

This invention of Molly's is just one of the innovative things about her. She also created, through the PA Government Schools held in the summer, the very unique Sleepover Shakespeare Society, a group of ten girls who meet once a month and have dinner and a sleepover—all centered on a certain Shakespearean play. They discuss what they've read, then either do a skit or parody from it or create their own video. They met for almost a year and when they were done, younger sister Hannah stepped in once again and ran it for another year.

According to Molly, her homeschooling started in the womb. She learned how to read when she was three by looking over her mother's shoulder as she taught her older brother to read. Although her instruction came from a variety of resources, Molly doesn't care for the term. "I don't like the term 'instruction'. I think it applies better to conventional schooling. Rather than being passively instructed," continues Molly, "I learned actively, and my parents, the Internet, a college class and my own initiative all served as guides to help me learn."

Initiative, Not Instruction

Molly has two older brothers, Jesse, 25 and Jacob, 22. Jesse is a grad student in a doctoral program in Political Science at Carnegie Mellon University. Jacob just graduated from the same university with a degree in Computer Science and is now working as a programmer for a large computer software company. Younger sister, Hannah, 16, is still at home and in 10th grade. All four of them have been homeschooled from the very beginning, all the way through high school graduation. Susan's first introduction to the concept of home education was over 20 years ago when her first child was two. "We were visiting grandparents for the holidays and I happened to catch John Holt on a talk show," she recalls. "My sister said that this guy was 'into homeschooling' and my initial response was: 'What a crazy idea—but interesting.'" By the next year, Susan's attitude had shifted and she was beginning to look into the concept. Her biggest hurdle was her husband, Howard. "My husband was a former teacher and had a Ph.D.," she explains, "and had worked as a reading specialist. He was completely against homeschooling and I had to work on him for about a year. What finally convinced him was he realized that with little children, you can't go back and rewind if something goes wrong—it's a one shot deal."

Susan's flack for her unusual decision didn't end there. "My mom didn't talk to me about it for three or four years," she explains. "Finally, when I asked her about it, she said she had suspected that's what we were doing." Disapproval was clear. "Eventually, we won her over though," says Susan. "The kids sent

Chapter Six

her thank you cards, drawings, copies of the books they made and our family newsletter. She showed them to her Bridge friends and within three years, she was a great supporter."

Susan is a former teacher but says that she was a misfit in her chosen profession. "I came to being a teacher somewhat backwards," she says with a grin. "I read about alternative schools first, so I had a hard time with 'regular' schools. I liked learning with my kids, because I enjoyed their company immensely and found it a great adventure. Homeschooling gave me a chance to do what I really wanted to do."

Molly's curriculum, like that of many homeschooling families, shifted with time. In the beginning, thanks to the influences of authors like John Holt, Susan chose a child-led learning style. "I was certainly influenced by educators who favored a creative approach full of real books, authentic writing for real purposes, real question raising and being a learner along with your children," she says. In the early years, the family made sure they had lots of terrific resources and books and for some years, several of their kids had writing projects going. "Our kids put out their own newsletter for several years and Molly began a hysterical little newspaper called *The Pet Periodical*, written by our pet, telling of all the intrigues of animal life on our farm."

Molly's family spent a lot of time reading out loud, talking, wondering and going places. They used a combination of materials from field trips to workbooks to simple life activities. "We had lots of art materials and hung out kid's pictures everywhere in the house, at least in all the places where there weren't books or displays of animal bones and deer antlers we'd collected in the woods or

Initiative, Not Instruction

unicycles hanging from big hooks from when the kids learned to ride them." Molly sees a huge benefit to homeschooling. "It taught me to be curious and proactive in my education. I didn't learn to study simply for tests; I studied mostly because I wanted to. Homeschooling also taught me to be independent, socially and intellectually. I don't feel the need to think or act in a certain way because everyone else thinks or acts that way," she says.

As the children grew older, there were some natural shifts in curricula. "By high school, we were looking to create a unique program that was also strongly college prep and would allow our kids to really stretch themselves and meet high goals," says Susan. "Our philosophy grew up and changed as our kids did." Record keeping changed and the family always kept some 'free form' within their stricter routine.

Homeschooling began to focus more on academic and art competitions and major projects, finding summer opportunities away from home and taking advanced online classes. The family's level of involvement in homeschooling took a leap over a decade ago when Susan and Howard formed the Pennsylvania Homeschoolers Accreditation Agency in 1991. PHAA is a non-profit, state-wide homeschool membership organization that helps provide legitimate diplomas to homeschoolers and find scholarships. Beginning with just six graduates their first year, they had over 500 in 2001. The family also produces a quarterly newsletter called *PA HOMESCHOOLERS*™, which Molly edits. It helps to link the homeschoolers throughout the state. Susan and Howard have also written a number of homeschooling books, including *The Three R's at Home*, *Writing from Home*, *Story of a Bill* and *Math by Kids!*

Chapter Six

Socialization was never a problem with Susan and Howard's family. One of their favorite activities for the last decade has been their monthly homeschool square dances. Susan plays guitar while Howard plays the fiddle and provides the calls, but just recently they had to stop hosting them. "I'm a bit sad to see that era end, but it was time for all of us to move on," explains Susan. "We're probably going to do more with square dances for other homeschool groups in our greater region, however."

When Susan reflects back on her years of homeschooling, she does say that she wishes they had made an effort to go beyond the homeschooling community for social interaction—especially places that would understand and support their Judaism. "Our family is Jewish and we didn't know any Jewish homeschooling families in our region. We were not at all associated with the Pittsburgh Jewish community or a synagogue. This has changed completely for my younger daughter Hannah. She has a nice core of friends from our synagogue and through other Jewish education classes for teens. It is very important to find friends within your own religious identity." Molly agrees. "I would have liked to have had more exposure to Judaism growing up," she says. According to Susan, the lack that Molly had in her high school years is improving now that she is in college. "She has access to a vibrant Jewish community in Pittsburgh."

Getting into college was an easy process for Molly, who is a Chancellor's Scholar with a full academic scholarship for five years in the honors college at the University of Pittsburgh. This scholarship is based on a combination of SAT scores, essays that

Initiative, Not Instruction

demonstrate the unique personality of the student and one-on-one interviews. Only about 18 students receive this honor each year—and over 6000 apply. "Remember that many colleges are just as interested in the fact that you milked goats or tapped maple trees as they are in your G.P.A. and other statistics," says Susan.

Today, Molly is a junior and has a boyfriend and is hoping to go to graduate school in psychology and linguistics so she can one day move to Israel and teach English there. "Some of my courses in college have been very simple because I learned the material in high school or before," she says. "When I took statistics, for example, I realized I already knew a lot of its concepts from a project about the probability of drawing certain colors of M&Ms® from the fifth grade!"

Susan wasn't surprised to see Molly go the college route and succeed. "I saw Molly as someone who would probably find it a bit challenging to decide upon a major, as she is very able and interested in many fields—art, languages, different cultures, writing, literature and psychology. I see her wanting to continue to travel and be involved in teaching. I see her as someone who will really value marriage and homeschooling her own future children if it seems the right thing for her family. As far as particular jobs she might take on fulltime after college," continues Susan, "my vision is a tad hazier. My guess is that she will find some unique way to combine her interests and work in something that is meaningful to her."

Chapter Six

Susan's predictions for Molly's future include a deeper involvement in Judaism and the Jewish community, increased fluency in Hebrew and some publishing of her writings. "I think that she will be very happy, kind and creative," she adds. "As Molly moves on well beyond the 'nest', she is still one of my favorite people to be with. It's absolutely remarkable to find that your kids turn out to be real individual people who you like, value and cherish and who are moving ahead in their lives." She sends advice to the parents who are contemplating homeschooling through the teen years. "Teens are wonderful people," she says. "The possibilities of in-depth conversations, really fascinating research projects, seeing your kids go way beyond what you know and can do, while still maintaining a core of family closeness, have all been really special. Don't be afraid of the teen years. This is the time where they are discovering who they really want to be and it is wonderful to be there as they sense their life direction!"

Chapter Seven

Bryan—A Mother's Decision

Bryan was lucky; his mother had already made a decision long before he was born that would make his life easier, happier and better.

Before she even had any children, Susan was already leaning towards homeschooling. Because she had an elementary education background, she had studied public education and discovered enough to recognize that public schooling was not what she wanted for her children. "I happened across a homeschooling book and I was hooked," she says. "It just made such good sense

Chapter Seven

to have education be a part of life and to be able to fit learning to the child, rather than the child fit the learning. I wanted learning to be natural and exciting, not boring and a chore. I love learning and homeschooling sounded like great fun because I could learn right along with my kids. The closer I got to actually starting, the better I felt. I figured I would just take it one day a time."

When Bryan was just about six years old, his mother began to notice some odd behavior. "He made strange sounds and jumped around quite a bit," she explains. "He blinked his eyes and cleared his throat or coughed constantly. He would scream in the middle of a conversation, or apologize to furniture when he bumped into it." In addition to these unusual symptoms, Bryan was also jerking his head quite a bit. Susan was concerned and so, like most mothers, took him to the doctor to see what might be wrong. The physician's advice was nothing short of insane. "Don't worry," he told her. "There's nothing wrong with your son. Just send him to school and when the kids tease him enough about his actions, he will stop."

This certainly wasn't the answer Susan was looking for. For two years, she looked for a diagnosis for her son's abnormal behavior. Finally, she read an article in a magazine that described a condition that seemed to mirror her son. "I made a list of his symptoms and went to another doctor," says Susan. "I had to talk him into it, but finally he referred me to a pediatric neurologist. I told him I believed that Bryan had Tourette's syndrome and he agreed." Bryan was given medication for several years. While they helped with the worst of his symptoms, they also made him quite drowsy. Occasionally, Susan or Bryan would forget to take his medication and nothing happened. The symptoms didn't get

A Mother's Decision

worse but Bryan felt better. By the time he was 10, Bryan decided to quit taking the medication, feeling that he would rather put up with any symptoms that the numbing from the drug.

Susan well knows what would have happened to Bryan if he had been in school with Tourette's. The negative socialization could have been devastating. "I know he would have teased a lot for years," she says. "With homeschooling, he was able to retain a good self-image, despite the tics and obsessions."

There were other reasons that Susan chose to homeschool, of course. One was the issue of faith. "Religious reasons became more important as time passed," she explains. "I liked being able to insert our family beliefs and values into the curriculum, to present other sides of an issue that schools would not be able to present and to have Bible study as part of our day together." Along with this issue, Susan also knew that her sons learned in different styles and paces and with homeschooling, she was able to work with that to their individual advantage. "Bryan learned how to read on his own by age five," she explains, "and would have been bored stiff in kindergarten and first grade. My second son didn't learn to read until age nine and would've certainly been put into remedial reading. He would have been made to feel stupid, whereas now he is a top student because he was able to wait to learn to read until his brain was ready. In many areas," she continues, "I found my boys could quickly catch up to 'grade level' once they were ready, while trying to force it earlier resulted in very little actual learning."

Both Bryan and his younger brother were homeschooled from birth. In the early years, Susan chose to use a rather informal style, with unit studies that tied different subjects together.

Chapter Seven

As the boys got older, however, that changed. "We felt more of a need to be structured in the high school years," she says. "We followed recommended classes that would look good on a transcript since both boys wanted to go onto college. The importance of record keeping increased greatly." Because both of her sons were planning to go onto higher education, Susan believed that her homeschooling needed to be more formal. She documented his activities more and tried to plan coursework that would appeal to the colleges that Bryan would most likely apply to.

"I did feel really nervous about the looming specter of college," she admits. "I was worried that I might forget something essential in his education that would keep him out of good colleges, that somehow I would ruin his chances through poor record keeping, or not enough of the right classes or references. It was scary," she continues, "because I felt during the high school years, I really held my son's future in my hands. I hadn't felt that so strongly before. What helped most was others who had gone before and who helped me through books and emails. Seeing others successes gave me the courage to forge ahead."

Originally, Susan thought that Bryan would attend high school full time but the closer the time got, the less she thought this was a good idea. In the end, the decision was up to Bryan. His decision was to go, but only part time. He took a number of classes, including computers, P.E., physical science, English, biology and algebra. In addition to high school classes, he also took classes at the local community college. There he took a wide variety from taekwondo to Japanese to astronomy. Since not all of his Tourette's symptoms were gone, socialization was still an issue.

A Mother's Decision

"It was a little rough at first," he admits, "but by my sophomore year, I was getting along well with people." His mother agrees. "A couple of times kids teased him or looked at him funny and tried to imitate the sounds he was making," she says, "but he learned how to cope with it. He just told them that he had Tourette's and they left him alone." At home, Bryan studied English, history and foreign languages.

Like many homeschoolers, Bryan split his time between classes and other activities. "I worked part time for awhile at a computer forensics lab in my sophomore year," says Bryan. "It was a company where I learned how to search for things in computer files all over the county, as well as search people's computers for illegal information that they had tried to hide or destroy." Bryan also had an internship at a plant which makes computer chips and semiconductors. "It was a really boring job," he says. "I had to take readings of airborne particles every three to four feet and make graphs of what I found. I also had to check for cracks in seals and filters." Along with these jobs, Bryan participated in a Japanese exchange program and a Science Bowl team. "I wanted him to have opportunities to interact with others in small group settings, activities that reinforced our religious and moral values and activities that helped him discover and nourish his passions," says Susan.

Coordinating the various schedules of her son's work, public school, community college and homeschooling was a bit of a challenge for Susan, of course. Sometimes managing it all meant something else had to go. "Since Bryan was in public school part time" she

Chapter Seven

explains, "our family had to make arrangements according to their schedule and fit our activities around it. That meant an end to our September camping vacations, which saddened us all."

Today, Bryan, 20, is going to his mother's alma mater, Stanford University. Getting into college was no problem either. Susan and Bryan got information online on how to write a transcript and that, along with a list of course descriptions from his classes at home and his public school transcripts, made the process fairly simple. Bryan is studying a unique combination of Japanese and aeronautical engineering. "I am doing research on experimental space and aircrafts," he says in an excited voice. "As for Japanese—I like it. It's the best language to use in the high-tech field." Bryan plans to graduate in 2005 or 2006 with a Master's degree and will, most likely, find an engineering job and then work on his PhD. Currently, he lives in a relatively small dorm with 56 others. The dorm is called Narnia, from the C.S. Lewis series of books, and it is small enough that everyone knows each other and does things together.

"Bryan has always loved to build and design things," says Susan, "so his goal to be an engineer is what I expected. I imagine he will also do a lot of traveling, especially to Japan. I am very proud of how he has set goals for himself and then worked to fulfill them," she adds. "I am also proud of how he has stuck to his religious convictions, even in a school where they are not necessarily the norm."

"The teen years are the pay off years," concludes Susan. "After all the training and teaching and learning together, I finally see my boys developing into fine young men with high standards, questioning minds and wonderful personalities. They are great people to spend time with and I would have missed all of that if I had sent them off to school. Instead, we are still friends and they look to my husband and I for advice and encouragement. There are challenging days, and it can be work, but it's worth it." Her son agrees with her. "Allow your teen to grow," he advises. "These years are when a lot of people start figuring out what their real interests are. Encourage them—if they are reasonable—even if they want to be an artist when you have always dreamed of them being a doctor or a rocket scientist."

Chapter Eight

A Trio of Unschoolers

When it came to interviewing this family, it is impossible to decide which of the three daughters to write about. Each one is unique and fascinating and together with their warm, open parents, the trio makes up the kind of homeschooling family that would make for an accurate documentary on unschooling.

Devin and Maria have three girls—Courtney, 21; Erin, 18 and Alyson, 17. They also have a stepson who left school at age 16 and defies that traditional image of a high school dropout. "My stepson Demian decided to leave public school about the time we decided to homeschool our daughters. When he made that decision, his arguments made sense to us and we were okay with it," says Maria. Contrary to that typical picture of a dropout, spending his days working a dead end job and deeply regretting his decision, Demian began apprenticing with a client of his mother's (a graphic artist) in a recording studio and taking classes in recording at a community college. "In about six or seven months, he had learned the whole business," recalls Maria. "He was paid to set up sound systems and quickly became known as one of the best sound man in the city." Now, Demian, 32, is married and has his own high-end cabinetry business.

Chapter Eight

The concept of homeschooling originally came from Devin. "He was always bored in school," says his wife, "and he just wasn't intellectually challenged. His mother wouldn't let the school move him ahead for social reasons." In 10th grade, he had had enough. According to Maria, he went to a new school one morning, following another family move, and when he walked into class to register, he was told he didn't belong there. With a deadpan face, he responded with, "You're right" and he walked out, never to return.

"Both Devin and I went to many different schools growing up," explains Maria. "It seemed to contribute to a general feeling of not being completely grounded in the system. It wasn't my idea to not send our kids to school, however," she adds. "He first mentioned it when I was pregnant for our first daughter." Although Devin was sure homeschooling was a terrific idea, Maria wasn't so positive. "I felt that schools placed too much emphasis on conformity and tended to discourage an inquisitive mind," he explains. "I wanted my children to be free to learn those things that interested them the most." Thanks to Devin's encouragement and support, Maria soon agreed with him. "He gave me the courage to acknowledge and honor my own natural learning process," she says. "He empowered me to learn what I needed to learn and gave me the space to explore myself."

Both Maria and Devin did a lot of reading in the coming months in order to help clarify their mutual vision for their children. "Our primary reasons eventually became to make sure our children always would love learning, that they would be empowered with certainty in choosing their paths; that they would be

A Trio of Unschoolers

free to be children when they were children and that they would not be forced from home at a young age to sit in a learning factory where everyone is taught the same thing and encouraged to do things the same way," says Maria.

In the beginning, like many parents new to homeschooling, Maria and Devin chose a more structured style of teaching, although somewhat more child directed than others. "We got worried that we needed to 'do' more," says Maria with a laugh, "so we tried to create curriculums. Our first daughter enjoyed it, but the other two were not at all interested. Courtney was a sponge but Erin and Alyson hated workbooks." Worry also entered the picture when nine-year-old Erin still did not know how to read. "I thought I was a failure as a parent," says Maria. "I went through psychotic episodes where I was sure that I had to start *doing something*. It would last for one day and then we would be back to make believe and creative play."

Fortunately, this stress came to an end when the family attended a homeschooling conference where they were introduced to the foreign concept of unschooling. "We were truly challenged by the thought of unschooling," she recalls. "It took time to dismantle the conditioning we had of what education was 'supposed' to be. In fact, it took several years."

A common experience for many homeschoolers are questions and looks from people who range from curious to hostile about their decision to homeschool. Devin relates two times when he faced challenges. "About 10 years ago, Maria and I were at a party that had a number of attorneys present," he says. "One them found out I was a homeschooler and proceeded to interrogate me.

Chapter Eight

He was definitely on the attack. There were also many times with Courtney where a clerk would ask her: 'What grade are you in?' We hadn't developed any kind of cover story at that point," he adds with a chuckle, "and so we didn't know what to say. We didn't use grades."

If their children are evidence, unschooling was a perfect choice for Maria and Devin to make. Courtney, the eldest, is currently living in her own place with her boyfriend, Brian. It's her first time living away from home and as she puts it: "It gives you a huge sense of responsibility but it's such fun for me. I always knew I would love living alone; this way I can create what I want on a blank slate." She attended college for three years which was just what she needed to satisfy her curiosity. She has a lot of experience in designing web sites for companies and still obtains most of her regular income from that. However, her newest venture may eventually take over the web designing. A few months ago, Courtney began her own organic produce co-op. It has about fifty members so far and ties in perfectly with her raw foods/vegan lifestyle. "This is the first time I've had my own business," explains Courtney, "and I felt an intense desire to find something to do with my life that has real meaning to it."

When Courtney looks back on her education, the pleasure in her voice is evident. "The greatest benefit to it all," she explains, "was the way in which I studied what was of interest to me. It was all about learning how to think and figure things out for myself.

A Trio of Unschoolers

Another benefit was developing an early appreciation of being different from most people; the strange and uncommon path I've been on my entire life has always had a sense of importance for me. I always knew it was the way I had to do things in order to have a true sense of satisfaction in life."

Finding friends wasn't a problem for Courtney. She was involved in ballet and competitive figure skating and had both homeschooled and public school friends. She and her sisters have spent time volunteering at the city's zoo in the children's section and she has also held several jobs. "At times," she explains, "especially during the preteen years when everyone seems to go through some degree of wanting to fit in, it was somewhat challenging being so different from other kids, but I got used to it and most important of all, learned how to relate to people in ways other than school—like common interests or human experiences."

Much of Courtney's education came from the Internet and books. "You can learn anything in the world," she says, "as long as you know how to read and how to search for answers to your questions." With the child-directed philosophy of education, kids are often learning things on their own on a regular basis. "It starts becoming important to figure out some things on your own and I spent much of my teen years more focused on coming into my own, learning about myself and the way I deal with things and less time asking for any outside help."

Chapter Eight

There's little doubt that Courtney is an advocate of the unschooling method. "My education and expertise are aligned with what has been of interest to me all during my life," she says. "Whether or not I know the dates of important historical events, know how to calculate this or that type of math equation, or can label each word in a sentence is irrelevant to me. If I ever come to see anything in those areas of study as something that is important to where I want to be in my life, I will be able to learn what I need to know easily. This is because I know the important part— I know how to learn."

Some of Courtney's thoughts on her life and education bring to mind a person who is much older—but she already has a head start on the 'wiser' part. "Growing up this way has allowed me to discover my true interests much earlier than most," she says. "Many people only find what they are truly passionate about when they feel like they are too old to do anything about it—if they find it at all. Instead of spending 12 years getting good at things that other people think I should be good at, I have had my whole life to explore my interests. I can only imagine what it would have been like if I had spent 12 years in public school. I imagine I would've had a constant sense of urgency like I was wasting my life."

After Homeschool
Fifteen Homeschoolers Out In The Real World

A Trio of Unschoolers

ERIN

Erin is the middle sister and the one who worried her mom because she wasn't reading. (The very first book she read was *A Wrinkle in Time*, followed by the Old Testament.) "My parents tried to get me to do some workbooks at first," she recalls, "but I didn't like learning that way. So, they gave me resources for what I wanted to learn. I mostly learn from life and my experiences and I don't consider my education separate from anything else in my life."

As part of her overall education, Erin has taken private music lessons and she plays violin in a youth orchestra. She too has worked at the local zoo in the children's section and has held several different jobs. Like her health-minded sister, Erin is a vegan and currently works at a health food market where she was recently promoted to the Customer Service representative. When she talks about the biggest perk of homeschooling, she doesn't hesitate. "The greatest benefit is growing up in the 'real world', instead of some institution that supposedly gets you ready for it," she states matter-of-factly.

Unschooling is a definite hit for her also. "Unschooling is the best. My parents allowed us to learn in the way that best suited the workings of our minds and in a way that fit our personalities. They didn't act like we were kids who had so much to learn but as people who came into this great world where there is so much to know and experience and choose from."

Chapter Eight

Since Erin is 18, she gets the usual question about when she is going to graduate. "I won't," she replies. "I will never stop learning. It's like retirement—you don't stop living, you just do different things with your time."

Future plans are up in the air at the moment. Erin and her boyfriend Lev share an apartment and hope to get married sometime in the future. Erin's biggest dream right now, however, is to be the violinist for her favorite band, *The Polyphonic Spree* in the UK. She recently attended one of their concerts and heard they had just lost their regular violinist. In typical homeschooling assertiveness, Erin followed the lead singer after the concert and asked if she could fill the position before they went on tour. "I may get to be part of my favorite band and tour the UK," she says in a voice that literally vibrates with enthusiasm. "I couldn't go to sleep until 5am, I was so excited. " Whether or not she achieves this dream doesn't matter— for Erin, there will be another one just waiting down the road.

A Trio of Unschoolers

ALYSON

The youngest daughter of the family is a 16 year old, very soft-spoken girl whose current passion in life is ballet. Her parents refer to her as 'the shy one of the family' but despite this, she has some definite opinions about her unschooled background. "I love it! I learn what I'm interested in. When the time comes when I need to know things I haven't yet learned, I can focus on those areas specifically. I have a great relationship with my parents and have freedom and time to do all the things I love the most." One of those things is dance. "I don't want to go to college," said Alyson who has been doing ballet for seven years. "I want to be a professional dancer in a troupe."

One thing that all three sisters agree on—and which brings a real sparkle to their voices—is Grace Llewellyn's Not Back to School Camp (NBTSC), as well as her book *The Teenage Liberation Handbook* or TLH. All three have attended the camp and read the book. "I read TLH when I was 17," says Courtney. "I already knew a lot of what it had to say but it inspired me to know I wasn't the only one with these radical ideas. It set off this overwhelming giddiness," she says. She went to NBTSC four times between 1999 and 2001 and says that she would love to go back for the rest of her life. "The place completely blows you away," she adds, "It left me speechless. I didn't know that that many cool people existed."

Erin agrees with her sister. "I went to NBTSC and I never realized there were so many homeschoolers in the world—much less open, creative, enthusiastic people—until I actually went to camp" Even Alyson has been to camp already—in 2000 and in

Chapter Eight

2001. "We had met Grace," says Maria, "and read her book and it changed our lives a lot. The girls got the traveling bug and began visiting friends in other states."

Some of the most telling words about homeschooling in his family come from Devin. "Being a guy, I have a different outlook on family—more protective than nurturing. I think it goes way beyond quality time to just *time*. The most important and satisfying accomplishment of my lifetime is raising and being with my children—far more than anything from work." In fact, in recent years, Devin has altered his work schedule so that he could be home far more than he used to. "I couldn't stand to be away like I used to be," he explains. "I listen to my co-workers talk about their cars, houses, money and ex-wives and they have no relationship with their kids whatsoever. They aren't happy. My kids are my best friends," he continues, "and I hope to be in close contact and communication with them all through their lives. I am just fascinated," he adds, "to see the rest of the story—the next episode."

Lastly, in a piece of advice he wants to share with other parents, he says, "As parents, it's our job to raise happy, loving, good human beings. I know that to some that sounds too ambiguous, too ambitionless. They think kids need roads that are clearly marked with road signs telling them exactly where to go and what to do at each step. However, our teenagers have learned that they are responsible for their own success and happiness."

Essay

Running Through Walls

by Cafi Cohen

(reprinted with permission from the author and from the May/June 2000 issue of Home Education Magazine)

Marathon runners talk about "hitting the wall." It happens about 20 miles into the 26-mile race. Despite months or even years of intense training, some runners find their energy and resources depleted just a few miles short of their goal. They cannot feel their legs. Vision blurs. Desire is there, but they think their bodies will carry them no further. They drop out. Other racers learn to run through the wall. They ignore what seems like an impossible situation and find a way to cross the finish line.

Like marathoners, most parents who homeschool children through high school also hit the wall. Their son needs to learn algebra or their daughter wants to study French. It happened to us when our son Jeff reached age 13 and announced that he wanted to learn to pilot an airplane. Both my husband and I avoid flying whenever possible so the thought of helping Jeff earn his wings appealed to neither of us. Because we lacked interest and knowledge, we hit the wall.

After Homeschool
Fifteen Homeschoolers Out In The Real World

Running Through Walls

At similar points, some families seriously consider discontinuing homeschooling. Parents fear tackling geometry, chemistry or Spanish, and they enroll their teenagers in school. Take Marta for example, both she and her husband confess to severe math phobia. Now their 15 year old son, having mastered arithmetic, including fractions, decimals, percents, exponents and square roots—is ready for algebra and geometry. Marta dreads the thought of opening an algebra text.

Joyce finds herself in a similar position—not because of lack of expertise, but instead because of a lack of equipment and facilities. Joyce is a retired nurse and her husband Jim is a practicing physician. They feel confident doing biology, chemistry and physics at home—except for laboratory experiments. How will they explain teaching a "lab science" on college applications?

Elizabeth and Bob face a different challenge. Like Joyce and Jim, both have math expertise and love science topics. Elizabeth has a degree in biology and Bob owns an electrical engineering firm. Both were computer geeks before anyone knew what that meant. Their wall? Elizabeth explains, "While I love biology and look forward to dissecting fetal pigs on the kitchen table, I don't see how we can possibly cover writing and foreign language with our teenagers."

All of these families can learn from experienced home educators. Pick and choose from the following headings—ideas derived from the comments on various online homeschooling bulletin boards—and create your own bag of tricks labeled, "What to do when you hit the wall".

After Homeschool
Fifteen Homeschoolers Out In The Real World

by Cafi Cohen

Do We Need This?

Sometimes homeschooling parents worry about their ability to cover chemistry or physics or Latin or Spanish without first evaluating the need for the subject. Yes, you can blindly follow a typical high school sequence with four years of English, three years of math, a year each of history and geography and government, two to three years of science and some foreign language. Surprisingly, though, you don't have to follow a college preparatory sequence for your teen to succeed with college admissions, or in life, for that matter.

You say you and your teenager don't want to do chemistry? Then don't do it. If astronomy or meteorology or horticulture sounds more interesting, let that be your science. Does studying a foreign language seem like a complete waste of time, given your teenager's other pursuits? The answer is simple. Skip foreign language.

Experienced home educators say that if you decide to tackle a subject you find impossible or your teenager finds distasteful, make certain you have good reasons for doing so. Also exhaust all acceptable alternatives.

Self-Instructional Courses

Compared to ten years ago, home educators now have a wide range of self-instructional courses to select from when it comes to difficult topics. You can buy self-instructional books that teach everything from algebra to biology. Some of my favorites are the Wiley Publishers' Self-Instructional Guides on more than 80 topics from geology to grammar to Spanish. In addition, self-instructional computer programs on many topics now line the shelves of software outlets. Finally, online you can find self-instructional courses in everything from Spanish to music theory and many of them are free.

Running Through Walls

Self-instructional courses are specially designed for use without a teacher. The course teaches. You, the parents, play your role by signing checks and cheering on your child's efforts. While building an entire curriculum around self-instructional courses might prove tiresome, using these learning materials for one or two subjects works well for many families homeschooling teenagers.

Self-instructional courses provide a hidden benefit. Teenagers learn not only the course content, they also learn that—given the right materials—they can teach themselves, even difficult subjects that people think must be learned in a classroom. Completing self-instructional courses builds confidence and educational competence.

Just Read

This is a variant of self-instruction. One homeschooling mother explains: "We have shelves of books by creative people who have done it better than we ever could on our own. Our homeschooler learns science from real scientists—Mendel, who grew peas in his garden and Gerald Durrell whose first scalpel was a razor blade."

Community Networking

Find experts for difficult subjects all around you. Ask you friends, neighbors and relatives for help, and you will find that many enjoy difficult subjects, like writing, math, chemistry and even foreign languages. Ask for their advice, and many will offer to help. One homeschool mother reports that her teenagers became interested in running and received coaching from their uncle, who works with a high school cross country team. Another

by Cafi Cohen

homeschooling mom explains, "We live in town with a population less than 700 and we still find resources galore. Our small church has a jazz musician, an accountant, an artist and older citizens who have lived history. plus, our pastor knows twelve languages and has a passion for ping-pong."

Beyond your immediate circle, explore community groups and classes. The sky is the limit here. Our son studied electronics with a local amateur radio club. 4-H Clubs sponsor Dale Carnegie public speaking classes. Church or community education classes may offer Spanish or American Sign Language.

Many homeschooling families enroll their teenagers in junior college classes for biology or chemistry or physics. The only real difference between college science classes and challenging high school classes is that the college classes move more quickly and go into subject in more depth. Once homeschoolers understand this, many complete "difficult' college courses in their mid-teens. As our son pointed out when he took community college geology as a 15 year-old: "They started right at the beginning. If you could read and do basic math, you could handle this course."

Co-op It

Sometimes parents homeschooling teenagers pool their efforts and form successful co-ops to handle difficult subjects. A homeschooling mother in Missouri writes: "I set up a homeschool high school co-op. We began with just band, drama and art classes and started with 30 children. Now we have 110 and offer biology labs, microscope labs, drama, choir, bank, jazz band, Spanish, five art classes, home economics and more. We filled a real need and the co-op has

Running Through Walls

succeeded far beyond our expectations. I'm thrilled because I had no intention of cutting up a cat on my kitchen table!"

Co-oping works even on a small scale. One homeschooling mom with three girls gets together monthly with another mother and her daughter simply to discuss the books they have been reading. All involved look forward to the activity and it has spurred interest in reading a wider variety of fiction and non-fiction.

Volunteering

Another family solves the foreign language challenge with volunteer work. The mother writes: "Our homeschooled teenage daughter works with children in the Head Start program. Most of the children speak Spanish and very limited English. They learn, she learns."

Our daughter learned both science and drama as a volunteer. For science, she volunteered for a year at a local veterinary clinic. She took vital signs on cats, dogs and horses; made up inoculations; learned to identify common parasites and watched biopsies and autopsies. She had a far better lab science course than anyone attending the local high school. For drama that same year, she worked as the property manager for a local community group and they staged a quality production from which she learned a great deal.

Tutors

Occasionally homeschooling families hire private tutors. This can be an expensive proposition. Even then, sometimes it is worth it to get through a brick wall. To find cost-effective tutors, contact the subject offices of any local college. Contact the physics department for a physics tutor, the French department for a French tutor and so on. Often they can recommend undergraduate or graduate students who will work for a reasonable fee. These are just a few ideas. Yes, you will hit the wall, indeed you may hit many walls if you homeschool your teenagers. And, like many families who have preceded you, you will find that you can climb obstacles or even run through them. The only people who don't make mistakes are those who don't do anything.

After Homeschool
Fifteen Homeschoolers Out In The Real World

by Cafi Cohen

*Cafi Cohen, homeschooling mother emeritus, educated her son and daughter at home through high school. She has written articles and columns for numerous national homeschooling magazines, in addition to authoring three books: **And What About College? How Homeschooling Leads To Admissions to the Best Colleges and Universities; Homeschooling the Teen Years;** and **The Homeschoolers' College Admissions Handbook.** She retired from almost 10 years of speaking at state and national homeschooling conferences in 2001. With her husband Terry and dog Phoenix, she currently lives in Arroyo Grande, California. There, she teaches piano and hand bells full time and sees local homeschoolers everyday.*

Chapter Nine

Jordan—A Parent's Investment

John and Stephanie knew something was wrong when their nine-year-old daughter Jordan was spending four hours a night doing math homework—and yet still not 'getting it.' "It really was a defining moment," says Stephanie. "I realized that she was only remembering material long enough to take the tests. As soon as it was over, she would forget it and this meant she couldn't carry a previous concept to the next one. She was memorizing and not learning. We were up to 11pm every night and it was painful for everyone." When she turned to the teachers at the private school Jordan attended, she didn't find the help she needed. Instead, since Jordan was making straight A's in all of her classes, they just shrugged off her concern. Just don't worry about it, they advised. "I couldn't do that," says Stephanie. "Finally we just hit a wall and it was apparent something had to be done." The question was what?

Chapter Nine

Unlike some families, it was Dad who came up with the initial idea to homeschool. He had heard about it at work and thought it might be worth a try. He felt that God was telling him to do this, leading him to it. His wife and daughter didn't quite see it that way. "I thought he was nuts!" says Stephanie. "I was sure I wasn't qualified. I was also pregnant at the time and all I could think of was, 'You want me to do WHAT?'" Despite that reaction, John kept encouraging his wife and affirming his faith in her that she could do it. She finally trusted in both her husband and God that this was the right decision for their family.

Jordan, in the meantime, was also struggling with the idea. "Dad started it all," she says. "I really wasn't too keen on it because it forced me to leave my school friends behind. It was also hard for me to get the mom/teacher role sorted out." Stephanie remembers that tough time clearly. "There were more than few tears shed that first year as I stumbled through with a split personality, teacher from nine till three and mom the rest of the day. She didn't respect me—teachers were the smart people, not mom." It took a few months for both mom and daughter to get comfortable with homeschooling. "In six months, I had completely adjusted," says Jordan, "and I was making friends in the homeschooling arena. Now I love it and wouldn't have had it any other way."

A Parent's Investment

One of the hallmarks of homeschooling is that it always shifts directions as the family grows. Perspectives change, maturity develops, self-confidence makes its way in, albeit sometimes rather slowly. The majority of families, however, all make the same mistake. They start off just bringing school home; same routine, different building. For virtually all families, that just doesn't work. "When I first started homeschooling Jordan," explains Stephanie, "it was really hard. I was trying to 'do' school. It was like I had forgotten the main reasons that we had pulled her out—school was too structured and one size fits all. It doesn't," she continues. "I would call John at work and tell him that one of us would be alive when he got home—so he better pick which one."

Quickly, Stephanie realized that this wasn't working for her and Jordan and she had an insight into the problem. "I tried hard to be the tough, emotionally detached teacher that she had been used to for the past five years, but that's not who I was and it definitely wasn't what she needed. She needed her very emotionally attached mom, the one who loved her unconditionally and whose goal was not only to help her learn, but also to encourage her to love learning," she says. When Stephanie stopped trying to be her daughter's teacher and went back to being the mom who loved her child and wanted to be a part of her educational experience, things began to click into place.

After Homeschool
Fifteen Homeschoolers Out In The Real World

Chapter Nine

Help also came in the form of finding out more about home-schooling from other books and people. "I went to a Mother's Night Out and discovered there were many different ways to homeschool," recalls Stephanie. "I read Mary Hood's books and she became my hero. I learned you don't have to do school at home like I was. That was so freeing!" Jordan found that just getting involved in lots of activities helped her grow. "4H was an excellent program for me," she says. "It provided social interaction and I took classes in nutrition, photography and public speaking. I served as president and in other offices, which taught me key leadership skills."

Despite a decidedly rocky start, both mother and daughter turned into huge homeschooling advocates. They got involved in a co-op with more than one hundred families and it worked out wonderfully for them. "A co-op is fun for everyone and it helps the children to see they are not the only ones homeschooling," comments Stephanie. "There, Jordan could take the classes that I couldn't and/or didn't want to teach. That proved to be the best thing I ever did because it took some of the pressure off of me to be an expert in every subject."

While there, Jordan took lab sciences from teachers with degrees in those fields, writing classes, a geography class and art history. "I took a debate class too which culminated in my debate partner and I going to the Annual National Homeschool Debate Tournament," says Jordan. Stephanie adds, "By far, debate was one of Jordan's most valuable high school experiences. It not only

A Parent's Investment

taught her how to thoroughly research an opinion, but also how to present an argument in a controlled and respectful manner." As the Watsons settled into homeschooling, their preferences in curricula changed. "I became more confident about taking a relaxed approach," says Stephanie. "I am fairly eclectic. Classical when it comes to language arts and logic, textbook in math and relaxed in science and history."

Jordan's homeschooling stretched far beyond classes. Like many older homeschoolers, she spent time both as both a volunteer and as an employee. "I went on several mission trips with my church," says Jordan. "I had my first job for two years as the principal babysitter/mother's helper of another homeschooling family. I helped with the cooking, cleaning and schooling of the children while the mother was recovering from an illness. From 9th grade through my freshman year of college," she explains, "I worked part time for a youth/music evangelist whose office was near my home." There, Jordan did everything from secretarial work to research to working the product table at various national conventions.

Today, Jordan is a junior in college and will graduate in 2004. Getting accepted was little trouble. Jordan scored 1260 on the S.A.T. earning her a tuition to the college she had chosen for her undergraduate studies in Communications. "As it has been throughout her entire life, Jordan has exceeded our expectations," explains Stephanie.

Chapter Nine

"The transition from homeschooling to college was easy," Jordan says. "I glided right in, although I did have to get the hang of homework." Where is she going from here? She is considering doing her graduate work at the Berkeley School of Music in Boston in order to study song writing and production. Currently, she is working at a Christian radio station where she previously did a summer internship. "I work in promotions, handing out prizes," she explains. "I am the co-host for an all request show on Saturday night and a DJ in training." Her parents predict that she will pursue Communications and eventually go on to homeschool her own children.

Her younger brother, Schuyler (9) has been homeschooled since birth. "When you start homeschooling from the very beginning," says Stephanie, smiling, "you don't have the problem with respect. You are the hero!" Schuyler agrees with her. "I love being homeschooled," he says. "My sister liked to homeschool in her room but I like to do it wherever mom is!"

When the family looks back on Jordan's homeschooling experience, it is with great pleasure and satisfaction. "I especially appreciate that I was allowed to learn how to think for myself," says Jordan. "People always worried about me being sheltered. I was always aware of what was going on in the world, but I was sheltered from the negative pressures to compromise and conform. They also worried I wouldn't have enough friends, but that was never an issue because I had plenty. If anything, I had a bigger advantage over others that were in public school. I wasn't limited to any curriculum. If I wanted to learn about something, we just fit it into my lesson plan."

After Homeschool
Fifteen Homeschoolers Out In The Real World

A Parent's Investment

Both Stephanie and Jordan were asked the same questions the majority of homeschoolers get asked at one time or another. "I was asked a lot if I was missing something by not having football games, homecomings, proms, letter jackets and other things," explains Jordan. "I guess I can see how that can be an issue, but it wasn't for me. I saw that my friends were in an environment that, while it appeared to have an upside, it also had an incredible downside. I think that the hardest part," adds Jordan, "is always feeling like you are swimming upstream, fighting the peer pressure and negative reactions from friends and family. It is wearying having to always defend and/or explain what you are doing."

Stephanie agrees. "The most difficult issue we faced was the constant peer pressure from all of Jordan's public/private school friends. They were always trying to convince her that she was missing out." That included family, of course. "We lived in fear that either side of the family would call Child Protection Services on us any day," adds Stephanie with a chuckle. "They were convinced that our children would not have any social lives or go to college and I'm sure they saw us as crazy religious zealots."

Like other young adults her age, Jordan was able to go through graduation—only the homeschooling version. "A mom in our area plans homeschool graduations, complete with cap, gown, Pomp and Circumstance," explains Stephanie. "It is a very special ceremony with each parent giving a five minute admonition to their graduate. She also provides professionally printed diplomas for each graduate in a leather portfolio." When Jordan graduated, her ceremony even made it into the local newspaper.

After Homeschool

Chapter Nine

Jordan's enthusiasm for her education is inspiring and leaves little doubt that she believes John and Stephanie did a great job. "I received an excellent education," she says. "And it's not because I'm so brilliant; it's because my parents chose to invest in my life and make choices that would further my education. When I compare what I know to what my public schooled friends know, I'm amazed at what high schools don't teach these days. The public school system puts students at a serious disadvantage, and that forces colleges to dumb down the curricula to accommodate the increasing lack of knowledge in the academic areas."

"Homeschooling has given me confidence in my own abilities and a chance to become who I am, without outside pressures to become someone else," explains Jordan. "I have no idea who I would have become had I been placed in public school, but judging from the way some of my friends changed over the years from the pressure, I don't think I really want to know. I might have lost a lot of my core identity and would've conformed instead of becoming who God wanted me to be. I'd have been a follower, not a leader. I suspect I wouldn't have fit in and been one of those nerdy, outcast people. Now I'm not. I am loved unconditionally for who I am."

Both Stephanie and Jordan have advice for those homeschooling families who are just approaching the teenage years. Stephanie feels that the key to success is letting the young adult have a significant say in their own education. "I believe the worst thing you can do is make your teens feel like they have no control over their own lives. It has been my observation," she continues, "that it is usually the 'controlled' teen that rebels. This is the per-

A Parent's Investment

fect time to begin treating your teen as a young adult." Jordan agrees one hundred percent. "Let your teenagers be part of the educational process. Let them pick what to study. They are far less likely to rebel if you let them structure their own learning environment, within reason."

Jordan adds her thoughts for parents about homeschooling the young adult. "Just because they are homeschooled doesn't mean they won't struggle with having their own identity. All teenagers deal with that. Let them explore who they are, being careful to place boundaries where needed. Be understanding of your child," she continues, "and encourage them to pursue what they enjoy the most." As for some advice for the young adults themselves, Jordan adds, "Homeschooling is what you make of it. Try to keep a positive attitude and appreciate the fact your parents care enough about you to invest their lives."

Chapter Ten

Tim—A Reflection of the Family

Many of the families who make the homeschooling decision do so after reading piles of books on the subject. Not so in Tim's family. His parents made the decision—and carried it out—without ever picking up a book on the subject. "There was just too much information out there," explains Lynne, Tim's mother. "I would've been overloaded. Instead, I went by word of mouth from others." Lynne didn't even consult books to help her choose a curriculum. "I just bought one and then looked through it," she says. "It was almost always self-explanatory." Lynne and her husband Paul did however attend several homeschooling seminars that helped give them some guidance.

After Homeschool
Fifteen Homeschoolers Out In The Real World

Chapter Ten

Tim's family came to homeschooling the way a growing number of others have—dissatisfaction with their own educational experiences. "I was always frustrated in school," says Lynne. "I got decent grades, but the material never really sunk in. If I got stuck, I had no help. I wasn't bold enough to ask a teacher and my parents didn't do much of anything to help me." Lynne and Paul heard about homeschooling for the first time from Paul's mother. "She told us about it but she was sure when we actually did it, that everything would go wrong," says Lynne with a smile. "Once she began to really communicate with the kids, however, she changed her mind." Tim has been homeschooled since he was five and his sister Sophia, 11, has been also. "My parents wanted to be more involved with my education," adds Tim, "not just keep me out of public school."

From the beginning, Lynne knew that she wanted a Biblically based curriculum. "I prayed for guidance," she says, "and the Lord led me in the right direction. We were able to integrate the Bible into different aspects of school." To help support this decision, the family joined their church's homeschooling co-op. "I never felt alone that way," says Tim. "I made many other friends and it helped show me how to deal with non-Christians." Through the co-op, Tim took History, Writing and Science classes and the occasional Bible study class.

A Reflection of the Family

In addition to the church co-op, Tim took classes at the local community college, including German. He also enrolled in track and cross-country through the nearest high school. He ran both hurdles and sprints and lettered all three years in track. "It was a complicated procedure with lots of hoops to jump through. I was constantly having to tell the administration what I was doing and show them a list of my classes," says Tim. Lynne also provided the high school with a report of Tim's grades and activities each year. "I am really glad that I went to high school for sports," says Tim. "It helped me to witness better. I also liked being able to push myself harder. The more effort you put into something, the better you will do and I like accomplishing something." Lynne is also grateful that she included some public school classes for Tim. "I felt that it helped him to become familiar with the adjustments of dealing with another teacher's expectations and in preparation for college life," she explains.

Lynne's homeschooling style changed with time, as most families do. "We were fairly structured at first," she says. "We had hours and days laid out in certain ways and then as the children got older, they began to teach themselves more." While she chose a set curriculum for math, she used a variety of materials for the other subjects. "In the junior high and high school years," she says, "I began delegating the work more—which was good because I was in over my head."

After Homeschool
Fifteen Homeschoolers Out In The Real World

Chapter Ten

The older years can be challenging both scholastically and emotionally. "Junior high had its spikes and its low points," says Lynne. "There were times I thought I couldn't handle it—just those occasional horrendously bad days—especially dealing with hormones," she admits. "I found that the key was talking through things a day or two after the emotions have had a chance to cool off. It was difficult to balance my parental authority with Tim's growing need to be independent. Who was going to hold the reigns in different situations was a constant decision making process. However, I enjoyed watching Tim mature and although there were stressful times, they were overshadowed by the good." Keeping in close contact is one of the biggest advantages to homeschooling, according to Lynne. "The best part of it has been having such close communication with Tim because I'm really nosey," she laughs. "I wanted to spend time with him and learn all about him. He is such fun to be with!"

The feeling seems rather mutual. "I think that being homeschooled made me really close to my mom," he says.

The advantages didn't end there, of course. "Homeschooling gave me the chance to improve upon my weaknesses," says Tim. "It helped me tremendously to be able to try a lot of different things to see where I had my talents and where I didn't." Tim truly feels that flexibility is one of the major keys to successful homeschooling. "I wasn't contained like other kids," he says. "For fun, we would go on random field trips and choose what we wanted to do. We went on tons of field trips and if it was a nice day

A Reflection of the Family

outside, we could work outdoors or take the day off." Tim also spent some of his time working in a grocery store and he also was part of a Youth Group and the Civil Air Patrol. "I steered away from anything that might distract me too much," he says.

Prom and graduation, two typical rites of passage for the young adult, were not a problem in Tim's household, although one was rather stressful. Others invited Tim and some of his friends to the high school prom. Graduation was provided through the church co-op complete with robes and diplomas. Both students and parents took turns speaking and exhibits of each child from birth through the present were displayed. "There were six students altogether," says Lynne. "Tim really didn't want to do it because he didn't see the point of it. It was enormously stressful because each mom wanted to do it her own way."

Today, Tim is 18 and a freshman in a northwestern college. He is majoring in History and hopes to teach at the high school level. Lynne is pretty sure that he will graduate, find a job and eventually get married. "The sky is the limit for him," she says.

Preparing for college was easier than the family had expected. Lynne's first piece of advice to others is to box up all the schoolwork, curriculum and textbook lists they use for each year of high school. "It really helps when it comes time for filling out college applications," she says. It must have worked for her. "Mom came up with all the documents I needed to get into college," says Tim. "She had all the paperwork from the co-op and of course, I had information from the community college and high school."

Chapter Ten

"Homeschooling is a real reflection of a family's personality," says Tim. "I think that there are two pathways you can take. You can make homeschooling your family's way of learning with limitless options. You can do and learn just as much as you want to or are willing to do. Another way to go is making learning just your way of life. You need to set and fulfill your goals and realize that you are responsible for your work. Choose what is most important to you and your family," he adds, "and don't ever try to do it like someone else does. Make homeschooling your own!" Wise words from someone who has been there, done that and is making his way out into the world with gusto.

Chapter Eleven

Kim—Finding Hope in the Journey

In some families, it's the mother who first considers the possibility of homeschooling. For some, it's the father. In still others, it might be the grandparent's suggestion or a friend's or co-workers'. In Kim's family, it was none of the above. It was Kim's decision—and it wasn't a popular one. How unpopular depends on who is asked.

Kim had done well in elementary school and junior high, winning awards in math and science. "When I first started school, I loved it," she says. "I loved finding out about things, even loved taking tests. I made the

After Homeschool
Fifteen Homeschoolers Out In The Real World

Chapter Eleven

Honor Roll and was put into the Gifted Program." And then along came high school. "As the years went on, I began to hate school with a passion," she recalls. "I hated the way we were taught and treated, the atmosphere it fostered, the time it wasted. I was staying home at least one day a week feeling sick." At 15 years old, she was one miserable young lady.

Kim's mother, Sonia, remembers this difficult time well. "I would wake Kim up to go to school," she says with a soft Jamaican accent, "and she would cry because she didn't want to go and I didn't understand why. Was she being teased? What was wrong? I even called some of the people she went to school with to see if they could tell but they were clueless." Sonia was upset and confused. How could she help her daughter when she wasn't sure what was wrong?

"School was the first, last and heaviest straw in a chain of negative events for me. It was necessary to remove myself from that situation," explains Kim. "I knew that if I stayed in public school, within a few months, I would either run away or try to commit suicide. I honestly don't believe if I had remained there, I would have graduated—or even still be alive today." Kim's words are painful to hear and seem equally hard to share. Now and then, despite being raised in Florida all of her life, a word or two in her conversation will subtly echo the Jamaican accent of her parents. "I was very depressed in school and had no friends," she continues. "There is nothing like the loneliness of being surrounded by thousands of people moving like cogs in a machine in a windowless building to the sound of a bell."

Finding Hope in the Journey

Kim didn't know where to turn for help and her parents didn't know what to do, nor did they really realize the depth of her frustration and sadness. Just prior to going into high school, Kim's older brother Justin was killed in an automobile accident and Sonia wonders if that was part of her daughter's unhappiness. Kim doesn't think so.

As things continued to get worse, Kim found the book that her mother now calls the answer to her daughter's prayer. "If I hadn't stumbled across *The Teenage Liberation Handbook* by Grace Llewellyn in a bookstore one day," explains Kim, "I might have never discovered how easy and how sane it was to leave school. It was the very reason for beginning my homeschooling endeavor."

When Kim came across the concept of quitting school and homeschooling, she saw a flash of hope for the very first time. When she told her parents about it, however, they didn't quite see it the same way. "We hadn't heard of homeschooling," says Sonia. "We were both feeling very hurt and disappointed in Kim." Both Sonia and her ex-husband Herbert were born in Jamaica and moved to New York in their teens. "We were used to tradition and this idea was very, very new to us. We thought she should do it the usual way—go to school, graduate, get a job."

Kim remembers their reaction as being a little stronger than that. "We had some real screaming battles when I told them I wanted to homeschool," she admits. "They thought it was a terrible idea, but I don't think they realized how miserable I was and they couldn't make me go to school. What could they do? Kick me out? Call the police?"

Chapter Eleven

At first, it was rough going. Through researching the Internet, Kim found a homeschooling correspondence program that she enrolled in. It seemed like a compromise for her and her parents; a middle ground where they might agree. "Every day my parents would ask me, what did you do today?" she says. "If I didn't have the right answer, the next question would be what are you doing with your life?" Kim only stayed in the program for a little while, finding the structure of it stifling and unnecessary. While she believes that such programs work well for many, it was not what she wanted at all.

Today, Kim is 19 and has been unschooling for four years. Although her parents live in Florida, she currently lives in Oregon with some other homeschoolers. Her parents still don't approve of her decision but have come to a reluctant acceptance. "After we got over the initial shock of it all, I came to see that this is what my daughter wants so I try to support it," says Sonia. "Kim is very smart and knows how to learn a lot on her own." Despite this change of attitude, Sonia has never sat down and read an article or book about homeschooling; it is still a rather alien concept to her. "Mom's only experience with homeschoolers is me," says Kim. "All she knows is what I have done and the pictures and videos I show her."

"From where I stand now," says Kim, "I know that unschooling was the best possible decision I could have made. The greatest benefit of it all is freedom. The freedom to learn what you want when, where, how and with whom you want, depending on your goals. Algebra curled up on your bed, Music Appreciation in the

Finding Hope in the Journey

middle of the woods with a couple of talented friends, a political discussion on a bus in another country. There are no bells to interrupt my projects and I can always get up and go to the bathroom."

The young woman, who once had no friends at all, now has friends all over the country. Like so many other teenage homeschoolers, she went to the Not Back to School Camp (NBTSC) in Oregon and met more than a hundred other people just like her. "Here was a place that I could relate to people." From the moment she met the other campers, she knew what she wanted to do next. "I got a Rail Pass to ride the train and I traveled to California, Oregon, Washington, Canada, Colorado and Georgia," she explains. She has attended five sessions of NBTSC and spent half of 2001 traveling from one place to another. "Traveling is a great way to see interesting places, meet cool people, gain confidence, be responsible and have fun," she says. At first, traveling alone was a little frightening, but soon she was used to it. Her family wasn't so sure, believing that she was wasting her time and the money she had earned from working and saving.

Kim's opinion on making friends has deepened and matured. "I believe that homeschooling can lead to more fulfilling, interest-based relationships as opposed to the often superficial acquaintanceships that form when the only reason you interact with someone is because you're the same age and outside forces keep throwing you together. You don't have to worry about conforming to other people's ideas of who you should be because you can choose who to spend your time with. I realize that that is not always possible in the world at large," she says, "but if you have

Chapter Eleven

the option, why not take it? Being around supportive, genial people who aren't kicking your chair is a good thing, especially where learning is concerned. Homeschooling allowed me to be more of myself and helped me regain some of the confidence I had lost."

Most of Kim's learning, since she left school, has been self-directed. "I know she goes to the library and she reads all the time," says Sonia, "but I want her to take some classes to further her education so that she can get a job that pays her decently." Kim is a strong believer in being an autodidact, or self-taught learner. "I've never been formal with my self-education," she explains. "I learn mostly through reading books I buy or borrow—math, history, science, literature, tons of fiction, newspapers and magazines. The Internet is a great source of information on just about anything I want to look up—song lyrics, mythology, and Japanese pronunciation. I'm a sucker for documentaries," she continues, "and have watched many over the years. Lastly, music is one of the most important and prevalent things in my life. I consider it to be a very important part of my education. I also learn a great deal just by keeping my eyes open and talking and listening to people."

Her bottom-line regarding her education so far is this, "Why should everyone know the exact same things? I like knowing what I know. I'm confident in my ability to function in the world with what I know. If there's anything I'm not satisfied with, I can change it. What I do know for sure," she concludes, "is that because of homeschooling, I learned that I could control my life. The things I've seen and done, the places I've been—none of it

Finding Hope in the Journey

would have happened if I had stayed in school. I'm not as shy as I used to be, not so afraid to speak my mind or do what my heart says is right. I've been happier in the last few years than I have been my whole life." Sonia, who is still puzzled at her daughter's decision but also loves her, has to agree. "It all boils down to the happiness of your child," she says. "I want Kim to do what makes her happy."

Kim is quite interested in writing and music and she is also fascinated by different kinds of audio-visual possibilities and is rarely seen without either a camera or a video camera in hand. She has already made multiple home movies/documentaries of friends she has stayed with and traveled across the country to visit. She states that she hopes to one day pursue some kind of career in film/movie directing and is currently working part time at a Mexican restaurant.

Her satisfaction with her own path is more than obvious. She had words of advice to others considering following the same pathway. "Homeschooling during the teen years can be an amazing and sometimes challenging experience for all involved," says Kim. "Teens can truly spread their wings and find out what's out there. They have the chance to work on things that really interest them. Parents, don't sweat the small stuff," she advises. "Trust your kids and keep the lines of communication open. Remember, life is a journey, not just a destination."

Chapter Twelve

Carolyn—Making God a Priority

A few minutes on the phone with Colleen and her daughter Carolyn would bring a smile to most people's faces. They sound almost identical and both of their voices break into warm laughter very easily—and often.

Chapter Twelve

Chris and Colleen have been homeschooling for over a decade now. They have two daughters, Carolyn, 19 and Caren, 13. "Carolyn went to a private school for four years," says Colleen, "but Caren has been homeschooled from the beginnings. I didn't mess her up!"

When Carolyn was in elementary school, Colleen was shocked by the increasing amount of homework her daughter was bringing home. Each night was spent pouring over homework and doing drills for hours. This just didn't seem right, but what was the alternative?

The first time Colleen heard of the concept of homeschooling was from a woman at her church. "All I could think was— what an overwhelming task!" she recalls. "The thing that changed my mind was my own education." When Carolyn was young, Colleen had gone back to school to get an associate's degree in business. "Being able to teach myself this new material gave me the courage to teach my own children," she explains. As for husband Chris, he thought it was a great idea too. "That might have partially been gullibility," adds Colleen with a laugh.

Chris was in the Navy and often sent out for six months at a time. Homeschooling helped with the confusion of frequent moves. "I wanted to help our family maintain closeness and stability that our military life did not provide," says Colleen. Of course, the family had to adjust to the different requirements of the places they lived. Their ten years in Hawaii, for example, meant having to take SATs, submitting their schoolwork on a regular basis and waiting for the approval—or disapproval—in order to continue.

Making God a Priority

The guiding force behind this family's homeschooling, however, was always God. "I found that over time, homeschooling helped to instill in all of us a greater love for God," says Colleen. "He allowed us to continue to homeschool even after my husband retired from the Navy and we transitioned to civilian life. God enabled the finances to be available even during the lean times," continues Colleen.

Like the majority of beginning homeschoolers, Colleen started out quite structured, then relaxed as the months went by. "We would alter what we did almost daily," she explains. "Sometimes we would only school half a day then the next day, we might go extra long or put it off until the evening. We had the freedom to skip material that wasn't mandatory," she says, "and move along as soon as the topic was understood." She chose a homeschooling curriculum that fit her needs and her daughters, but it took a little trial and error to do so. "I heard of this new curriculum through a woman at church and it was more child-oriented than the one I started with. It didn't take a genius to master the teacher's handbook, which I liked," she chuckles. Carolyn approved of the changes too. "The first curriculum we used was too focused on teacher lectures, for my style," she explains. "I discovered that I need to read the material to myself and do it. This new curriculum was student paced; there was no need for lecture and I could do most of the activities by myself."

Chapter Twelve

As Carolyn and then later, Caren, approached teenage years, Colleen recognized their strong drive for some independence. "Chris and I tried to allow Carolyn to pace herself in her studies, while still completing the work necessary for graduation," she explains. "The other issue which required me to make an adjustment was her moodiness." The relationship that mother and daughter had already formed made this emotional roller-coaster easier for everyone to bear. "We had developed a relationship," says Colleen, "and I knew it would make it easier for her to come to me and be more honest about any problems. Perhaps, if she'd been in school at this time, she would have snapped at me or said something regretful."

During her teenage years, Carolyn played in a hand bell choir plus she stayed involved in church. "We felt it paramount that she attend a Christian church," says Colleen. "Faith in God is top priority. Next, we wanted adequate family time together because it you don't make the time, than many precious moments are wasted."

Carolyn is currently in college working on a degree in aerospace engineering. While she originally wanted to be an astronaut, her eyesight wouldn't allow for it. Now she is hoping to one day help build the spaceships. "She has been interested in astronomy since the sixth grade," says Colleen. "Her father and I assumed that she would enter the field of science." As Colleen looks back over the years her only real wish is that she had relaxed a little bit more. "I'm learning I can worry as much as I want, but it just doesn't change anything—except my stress level!"

Making God a Priority

When Carolyn reflects on her years of homeschooling, she is sure that her parents made the right decision. "I could spend time on my education and not conforming to my peers," she says. "I feel comfortable being me and not what everyone else wants me to be. I could work at my own pace and skip parts that were either too easy or irrelevant. I also had the chance to have a different—better—relationship with my mom," she adds. "Homeschoolers treat their parents way nicer overall."

Carolyn definitely bristles when she is compared to that typical teenage image of rebellious and difficult. "I resent comments like that!" she exclaims. "I'm sick and tired of everyone thinking that teens are recalcitrant and difficult! I tried to be as respectful and obedient of my parents while still trying to convey my desire for individuality. Teens want to be so independent—that's supposedly why they're rebellious—but then, why do they go around and wear the same clothes as everyone else, watch the same movies and believe the same ideas as their peers? How is this being an individual?" she asks. In reference to the stereotypical image of the teenager who can't seem to carry on a conversation with an adult-slash-authority figure, she says, "Teenage homeschoolers can often talk to people more than two years older than they are, without looking like a beaten dog because they talk intelligently!"

Another perk to Carolyn's homeschooling is the relationship that has developed between she and her younger sister, Caren. "We are like best friends," she says. "Because we moved around a

Chapter Twelve

lot, it was hard to find people to play with. I forced her to be my playmate and now she's my biggest friend. If we had both been in public school," she adds, "that wouldn't have happened. We would've both been too worried about what our peers thought."

Colleen sums up their family's homeschooling experience by saying; "The best part of all was spending time with our girls. My advice for parents who are just approaching this age is simple: Pray! Expect the child to change. It's inevitable that they will grow up, so let them! Give them extra responsibilities as you go and see if they can handle them." As Carolyn adds "Going through this age may be hard, but you will end up with an individual who knows what they really want to do with his/her lives."

Essay

Skydiving

by Jasmine Orr

I went skydiving this past summer. I'd wanted to do it for a really long time and my mother had never been very big on the idea. But last July, I made it to the magical age of eighteen where you can do anything you want. So I paid a ton of money to have someone fly me high into the air, open the door and shove me out. There was a 60 second free fall where I hurtled through the air, stomach doing these flips, not being able to breath quite right. Finally, there was a jerk as my parachute opened and I seemed to float almost motionlessly. I'd bet it was the most expensive ten minutes of my life; the adrenaline rush lasting at least five hours afterward.

Skydiving

It was an incredible natural high that put a grin on my face through the rest of the day. It was worth every dollar spent and the experience was breathtaking, the sort of memory that you will hang on to forever. It's a great conversation starter.

"What did you do this weekend?"

"Oh nothing... went skydiving."

And believe it or not, it even added to my so-called education. The way I've decided to build my education has nothing to do with classrooms, textbooks, grades, memorizing dates, tests, #2 pencils or any of the other things I associate with public school. Instead, every day that I live through, every person I meet, every experience I have is educational in a sense. Contrary to popular opinion, learning doesn't have to stop at graduation. It doesn't stop at the last bell. It's a lifetime pursuit.

I don't spend a moment with ordinary, planned out textbooks. I don't study anything for a second that I am not overwhelmingly interested in. I wouldn't retain any of it if I did so it would just be a waste of my time. Instead, I've learned to view my education like a collage, like life is just one huge magazine and my life has been spent going along with some massive cosmic scissors, clipping out the parts I want to keep, the parts I want to build myself out of, the memories I want to have. The outcome is a thousand times more colorful and useful than any textbook. By personal choice, I am following an insatiable urge to be like nobody has ever been before. I am concerned with the world's lack of originality and at times, I feel like I'm making up for everyone else's deficiency.

After Homeschool
Fifteen Homeschoolers Out In The Real World

by Jasmine Orr

I do everything for the experience of it, not the grade. Instead of buttons or seashells, I am a collector of experiences. That's why I jumped out of an airplane. That's why I've traveled all over the country on Greyhound buses and trains by myself. That's why I've talked to random people, read any books available, attended camps, listened to music from all the different genres, paid perfect attention to the world around me, held as many different jobs as I could get my hands on and studied a multitude of topics, devoting all my attention to studying something for a day, a week, 6 months... and then rapidly moving on to something else. Ever since I can remember, I've collected these things and ended up tossing them haphazardly into the box of my brain and letting them accumulate. I guess you could say that everyday is a classroom. I feel like I've gotten three lifetimes of experience in one regular school semester. I've got all the time in the world–and the best part is that it's my own time. It's like a permanent summer vacation but you've gotten enough of lying around and watching dumb sitcoms. You're ready to go out and achieve something on your own terms.

My life as I know it today looks like this; I work at the food court of the biggest shopping mall in Oregon. If you came by, you'd see me looking much like everyone else. I wear a color-coordinated uniform and I take out my nose-ring while I'm there and have refrained from dying my hair crazy colors. I listen to the same pop music radio station everyone else listens to and I know every word to every song by heart. I work with a staff of entirely

Skydiving

public schooled high school kids. I sell tons of cookies and soda. I plaster a big smile on my face when I step through the door and answer all the questions customers ask. Eight hours and three billion cookies later, I step out the back door, take off my nametag, let down my hair and relish being in light that isn't from florescent light bulbs overhead.

Through the service corridor and into the parking lot and I drive our '70 Chevy Belair home to the love of my life, Mitch and our charming little duplex full of an ever changing family of pets. (Currently, two mice, one rat, two ferrets and three cats.) There are posters on the walls, a stolen stop sign, a bunch of movies and a big mess on the living floor, that usually consists of half written poems, shreds of magazines and any random projects started and temporarily lost interest in. Mitch and I don't touch the radio but stick to listening to more unknown bands like Bright Eyes, Modest Mouse, Mates of State, Cursive or my all time favorite, Ani Difranco. We spend our days like anyone else–we just aren't obligated to spend most of our days cooped up in a building where we don't want to be, doing something we probably don't want to do. I'm eighteen now, technically not of school age anymore. Yet that doesn't mean that I graduated from learning but just from the expectation that I should be inside those four walls in which everyone believes you receive an education. In all honesty, I can't imagine how different my life would be if I had been made to spend my life inside those walls. I am very proud of the fact that I am more independent than that. Secretly, human beings are

by Jasmine Orr

allowed to do whatever they want. It's their minds to build. They aren't required to hand that responsibility to anyone else.

For years, I've had people ask me the question, "But how will you ever be ready for the real world?" I've never understood why I'm asked that because it seems to painfully obvious to me that I am IN the epitome of the real world. I didn't read about the real world first and then later, graduate into it. Instead, I was born into it and have grown up inside it. A random guy that I met while living in Indiana once took me aside when I was young and asked me with a totally straight face, "How will you ever learn how to answer the telephone or how to talk to people?" Even when I was that young, I knew how absurd a question it was.

Now that I'm out here in the big, bad world, I know that homeschooling has left me lacking nothing. I surround myself with situations that are worth my time and may be beneficial to my life. The best part is that I didn't have to wait to do these things–I began this process as soon as I was old enough to understand what I had ahead of me, the freedom and the opportunities. I was never forced to do anything. It was all self inspired. It was all inner motivation–not the advertised kind on posters in offices. I mean the real kind. Every moment I have is just another experience. My education isn't something that I actually think about much at all. Instead, it has been shoved into the recesses of my mind where it can do whatever it is that it does with all the things I pick up in life. The bottom line is that education is simply another word for the way I live my life.

Skydiving

There were turning points in my life. I started off answering the phone and making appointments at my dad's office when I was about nine. After that, I had tons of volunteer jobs, including the local library, the theatre and the animal shelter. Once I was old enough to work legally, I held jobs such as a clerk in a new age book and incense shop and in a music store, as well as a babysitter, lawn mower, waitress, camp counselor, dishwasher, outdoor educator and office organizer. At one point, I even went to Minnesota and worked at a Christmas tree and wreath nursery for a few weeks. They were all part time jobs, which grew to full time jobs, which grew into savings accounts that bought me bus passes and train tickets and suddenly I was set even more free.

I got hooked on traveling and every spare dollar was poured into the "get-Jasmine-to-a-new-destination" fund. One of the best trips was where instead of buying a specific ticket to a specific city; I just bought a month Greyhound bus pass. Basically, it allowed me to get onto any bus going anywhere as often as I wanted for a month. I made my way from Indiana to Minnesota to Oregon to Vancouver, Canada, back to Oregon, a few different stops in California, a couple cities in Texas, up to Wisconsin and back. It took five weeks but I was elated the whole time. I was only sixteen at the time and everyone I met along the way was amazed at what I was doing, that my parents would allow me to do it, that I knew people to stay with in all those states, that I could handle coordinating all of it by myself... and by the way, wasn't I supposed to be in school?

by Jasmine Orr

The whole time I was amazed myself because I had never even thought that other kids my age wouldn't be able to handle it. It was so easy! Being able to just jump onto whatever bus I wanted to, go anywhere I wanted to go and see all the people I never got to see? I carried around a battered road atlas and kept marking off cities and coloring in states that I had been through or stopped in and I adored every minute of it. I did lots of thinking and staring out the window and listening to music and writing. Thinking back on it, it was an experience that the majority of people will never have the chance to have. It was crazy sometimes–I was offered drugs, bus stations got moved across town without me knowing, my ATM card nearly snapped in half, I missed busses… and I still loved every second. It was all part of the exhilaration of traveling. When I tell people now about all the places that I've been, I'm saddened by all that confess they've never even been out of the city they were born in. I can't imagine who I would be now without going all over the place and falling into all sorts of adventures. After some borrowed money and some broken rules, I am now a happy little veteran of the United States. While I haven't gotten a chance to venture far and wide yet, I'm sure as soon as money and time allows it, I will.

One of my many past adventures was attending a summer camp called Not Back To School Camp. The journey to this camp was one of my first big trips. It was all the way out in Oregon—a long way from Indiana. The train ride took two days. I met a handful of people that were going to the camp as well and we hung out the whole time, eating junk food from the concession

Skydiving

stand and talking about our experiences so far. After two days on the train and two bus rides, I finally got to the campground and was in for a surprise because it was even better than I had expected it to be.

This camp was a crazy mix of people that were homeschooled or more often, the even more free "unschooled." It was a different attitude, or more aptly put, a different world from the schedule and rule oriented 4-H and Girl Scout camps of my past. These kids had wild dyed hair and they played dress up no matter how old they were. There were piles of cuddling at all times, talking and thinking out loud and staring at the sky. Everyone had the opportunity to teach a workshop on anything they wanted, which included anything from spray painting and massages to train hopping and capture the flag. The roles of teacher and student were disregarded and melted instead into the single role of human. I met some incredible people there that were doing amazing things.

My good friend Evan is still one of the people I trust and look up to most. He introduced me to music and ideas and ways of thinking that would have possibly never been a part of my life if not for him. Barely into his 20's, he's absorbed dozens of different projects, including becoming a marine biologist. Another friend of mine, Sarah, is a licensed pilot who is building an airplane, as well as playing a ton of musical instruments. Maggie is writing plays and actually seeing them produced in New York. Brent and Zen are in a band that is gradually getting more and more gigs. The

After Homeschool
Fifteen Homeschoolers Out In The Real World

by Jasmine Orr

people I met there are full of wonderful ideas and inspiration. Many great friendships grew from my experiences there, including meeting my fiancée, perhaps the most life changing and monumental of all.

One of the biggest turning points in my life was leaving Indiana and moving out to Oregon. Although my parents came to the West Coast also, I soon moved out on my own. It was one more experience to add to my collection... or a whole handful once you consider paying rent, having a full time job and an electricity bill. The West Coast is so open minded in comparison to my old town, it's incredible. Living somewhere that I don't have to explain what homeschooling is is great. Differences in lifestyles are normal here.

Honestly, if I were to document my experience in homeschooling completely, it wouldn't be entirely uplifting. There were times when I was angry because people were so ignorant about it, because public school kids my age ignored me, because the local homeschooling group was heavily religious and the fact that I don't believe in God banned me from the group. Thus, I was forced to spend a lot of my time alone—not because I was homeschooled but because of religion.

Once I was older, I was able to go all over the country and find plenty of wonderful people but it wasn't always that way. It is a reality that the kids in school weren't very nice to me, that going to Girl Scout meetings was awkward because none of the girls would touch me. I lived right down the street from the elemen-

Skydiving

tary school, middle school and high school and in the afternoons, when everyone was walking home, I stayed inside. Some days were filled with loneliness and disappointment. My uncle once sat me down and seriously asked me, "So, what's two plus two?' I was at least 14 or 15 at this point and I wanted to just walk away. Just because I can't reel off dates or recite the times tables, just because I'm not "text book" smart, doesn't mean I'm an idiot. People make so many uninformed assumptions about my lifestyle and some-how, won't listen to me when I try to explain the truth behind the way that I live. The truth is, yes, I do know how to read; I have been reading college level books since long before I was allegedly supposed to. Yes, I can get a job; I can even work anytime of the day, instead of just for a few hours after school. Yes, I can go to college; in fact, colleges adore homeschoolers because we already have a lot of self-discipline.

Now I'm settled into one place for the time being. I have a full time job as a supervisor in a bakery, I have an apartment, a circle of open minded friends and a wedding to plan. I have aspirations to follow my long time love of animal rights work and go to work with the ASPCA in New York City, although it might be a while before becoming a reality. I've been considering going to college for something but have no idea what it would for if I did. I go to concerts downtown and spend lots of time looking for new for-eign restaurants (I'm currently obsessed with Lebanese food).

by Jasmine Orr

I'm looking into being more active in causes I believe in, like vegetarianism. I'm still enjoying finally living on my own and being entirely in charge of my life. I'm in no hurry to accomplish anything in particular, which unfortunately can look like laziness to some. But the truth is, I've got years and years of experiences left to me, so why not? There are still so many countries to explore, people to meet, books to read, jobs to have and things to see. Every moment is full of potential. It has always been my choice whether to continue being homeschooled or to try school and I have always been sure of my choice to continue in my independence. My education will only be finished when I die. Only then will I be done collecting my experiences and only then will the collage that is truly me be complete.

Chapter Thirteen

Jake—Growing Up Great

When Cindie decided to homeschool her son Jake, no-one who knew her was really surprised. She had been a rebel for a long time and this was just one more step along the way. "I was a wild child," she says with a grin. "I did the opposite of what my mother wanted, moved out of the house at 17 and got my own apartment."

Two factors came together to make homeschooling look like a possibility to her. First, she had been really bored with her own schooling. Second, her son Jake was in serious trouble and she needed to find a solution. "Jake was so incredibly unhappy in public school," she says. "He would have stomach problems every morning, often bad enough that he

Chapter Thirteen

would throw up." He had reasons to be miserable too; four kids at school were assaulting Jake on a daily basis. They would steal his books, push him around and trip him as he walked down the hall. "The true irony of the situation," says Cindie, "is that Jake has been taking Karate since he was seven years old and he could have flattened any one of those kids. It's just not in his nature to fight." The school did nothing to help either. "Their response was to use 'peer counseling'," explains Cindie with a sigh. "As if a group of little hooligans are going to give a hoot about what one their peers had to say!"

To make matters worse, Jake had also been labeled learning disabled. He would spend part of his school day in a special LD classroom for help in math and reading. "That was the most useless time waster I've ever seen," says Cindie. "They taught him nothing and it was almost like they deliberately slowed his learning. He doesn't need a dumbed-down curriculum; he needs more hands-on learning, more independence and the opportunity to explore an interest until he's exhausted it." Cindie also felt that her son needed to move at a slightly slower pace than other kids, even though he was at the same level as they were. He needed more time to process the information.

Cindie prepared for homeschooling by reading a variety of books, including those by John Taylor Gatto and Ruth Beechick. She focused on learning style books and found them the most helpful. "Homeschooling styles kind of evolve with your family," she says, "and while it's helpful to read other people's suggestions on how they do things, it was more helpful for me to learn about my child learned."

Growing Up Great

Cindie pulled Jake out of school in his 7th grade year, at age 13. Jake remembers it well. "At that time, anything felt better than going back to public school," he says. "No offense to public school, it just didn't work for me. When I was in 6th grade, I was in an LD class because my math skills—to be perfectly frank—sucked. I felt really stupid because everyone in my regular classes was learning types of math I thought I would never learn. Sometimes when my mom dropped me off at school," he continues, "I raced back to the car and got back in and almost cried because I was so frustrated. I had low self-esteem and no confidence. I only had a few friends and most of the kids at school hated me. I met some very hostile people; they were mean. I never expected to be in a fight but I got into one with my former best friend," he recalls. "It was three against one and as they had me by the neck, all I could think was 'What am I doing here?' " Things went from bad to worse. "I had so many negative emotions I couldn't bear it," says Jake. "I was sad, angry, frustrated and confused. It all began to weigh down on me. One day, I just said, 'I can't take it anymore, Mom'. I buried myself in a pillow. All I wanted was to be happy!"

When Cindie proposed the option of homeschooling to him, Jake jumped at the chance. "My parents gave me options," he explains. "Homeschooling just felt right to me. I didn't need a hall pass to go to the bathroom and I could put my head down and relax if I needed to. The very first day, I enjoyed it!" he says. "I learned how great books could be. I improved greatly in math and my mom helped me in areas I was weak in. The rest I did on my

Chapter Thirteen

own." Before he began homeschooling, Jake had been tested to see how he was doing. "I was in below average," he explains. "After one year of homeschooling, I had already reached the middle of average and was still climbing! " Cindie agrees.

"When we started homeschooling," she shares, "the school hadn't even taught him to tell time past the quarter hour and he hated reading. Now he does math that is beyond my knowledge and I can hardly tear him away from the adult novels he reads." Favorites include the *Lord of the Ring* series, *Star Wars* books and anything about World War II.

Not that everything went smoothly at first. "Our styles are very different," explains Cindie. "I am very detailed and Jake sees the big picture from A to Z. I am still back on C." Cindie didn't believe that her son had any kind of learning disability either. "He learns in a different way," she stresses. "It's like he has an extra loop in his brain so it takes him longer to grasp something. He has to work with it, ponder it. A 45 minute math class dumbfounded him; he wanted to study it longer—so that got him labeled LD." Jake recognizes that he learns in a different style than many of the kids we was in class with. "I need silence so I can focus," he says. "I am a hands-on person."

As is typical with new homeschoolers, Cindie began with a very structured format. "I laugh about it now," she says. "I was so worried about giving Jake a good education. I wanted to make sure he hit every subject they covered in public school. I used the Internet, used reams of paper printing out lesson plans and spent hours figuring out what we were going to do. Jake, subtly, rebelled," she recalls. "If he didn't

Growing Up Great

really see a point in what he was doing, he just wouldn't do it. Hands-on science experiments worked, as did chats with NASA scientists. Curriculum was a bust. Finally, I just gave up." Cindie went through different styles of homeschooling as most families do. "We did school at home for one month," she says, "then we moved to total unschooling. Now we are more focused on college prep so we are using a set curriculum."

"It was hard to just let him go and learn on his own and follow his own interests," says Cindie. "One time he spent about three months playing a video game and I cringed. I felt so guilty—here he was, playing video games all day. Only to find out, he had been keeping a diary for his character. He had pages and pages of handwritten notes, some in a fantasy language used by the character about his life and adventures. That was a big lesson for me," says Cindie, "that things are not always what they seem."

Jake, now 17, has a new project similar to this underway. "I am writing down everything I learn in a little book of mine," he explains. "It's a good way to keep a document of what you've done and it makes me feel good when I look at the pages and realize how much I have accomplished." Jake's attitude towards like had changed dramatically through homeschooling. From total despair and feelings of inadequacy, he now says, "There are some areas I excel in and there are some areas that I need more work, just like everyone else. The fact is that I do know what I do well and not so well and I have the strength to better myself. This makes me feel happy and astonished."

After Homeschool
Fifteen Homeschoolers Out In The Real World

Chapter Thirteen

Jake is often asked the same question that all homeschoolers face on a regular basis: what about socialization? "People look for a problem in homeschooling," he says. "They point in a direction—like socialization—because they are scared or angry; they exhaust the topic and then the move on." Jake's only real problem when it comes to socializing seems to be finding time to fit it all in.

A look at what he does on a regular basis is enough to make anyone wonder how he manages it. Jake continues to take karate and just earned his black belt, and he gives karate lessons to younger children. He plays soccer year round for the local high school and is teaching himself Latin and Japanese. "The soccer team is absolutely fabulous," says Cindie. "The kids don't care if he is homeschooled, they just care if he can get the ball in the net. I don't know if the kids and the school would be so cooperative if he wasn't such a good player." In fact, Jake won Most Valuable Player in 2001.

In addition, there was his involvement in Destination Imagination, an international program. A team is given a long-term problem to solve and take it to a contest. Jake's team, made up completely of homeschoolers, designed an obstacle course in which six eggs were moved from one point to another without breaking and without even being touched by a human hand. It involved levers and other criteria and involved a professional presentation that blew the panel away. The team won first place in the world competition. It also was the first homeschooling team to win the prestigious competition. "It was a great confidence builder and really improved his creativity," explains Cindie proudly.

Growing Up Great

Ask Jake what his passion currently is, however, and his answer is clear—Civil Air Patrol or CAP, an official auxiliary of the US Air Force which is a civilian branch that has existed since December 1941. It encompasses three different areas: a Cadet Program, Aerospace Education and Emergency Services such as search and rescue exercises. "You learn about responsibility, team building and moral leadership," explains Jake. He has been involved since spring of 1998 and has gone through all three phases. "These are real meetings," he says, "where you wear uniforms and adhere to military standards and discipline." The group meets once a week for two-hour meetings and has camp outs, physical fitness nights and more. Jake is a Flight Sergeant in drills and hopes to have a future in the Air Force in either military intelligence or as a pilot. "Whatever he does," says Cindie, "I'm sure he will be successful. He has a tremendous work ethic and he is dedicated, disciplined—except for cleaning the pit he calls a bedroom—and very loyal."

Future plans have not been set yet for Jake. "He wants to go to college," says Cindie, "and is thinking about the military. He also really enjoys working with kids; he's wonderful with them and is thinking about child psychology. It's important to remember that society makes 18 the magical number to have your life all figured out, but that just isn't true. Jake will decide what is right for him when he is ready."

Chapter Thirteen

As Jake approaches this magical age and the end of his home-schooling, time is becoming increasingly precious. "I can count on one hand how many times Jake has ever been in trouble," Cindie says. "It has been so rewarding and it is such an important time for him. It's a really bittersweet time for me, though, knowing he will soon be on his own. Parenting is so full of clichés: first word, first step and so on. But every day of his life, I get to watch him grow into a man, to see his intelligence and compassion, his humor and his resolve. I can't imagine missing a minute of it."

Jake has some great advice for homeschooling parents who are approaching the teen years with their children. "Don't be concerned if your child doesn't want to learn something in a certain time. Let them learn gradually, at their own pace. Make sure there is always someone there. Prepare to learn yourselves because you will learn something along with your children."

What the last words from this assertive and articulate young man who once despaired of being stupid? "I have chosen what type of homeschooling I want to do and I know one thing—I am growing up to be someone great!"

Chapter Fourteen

Stephen—Living His Faith

Christina remembers the moment her family began their homeschooling journey quite clearly. "For a deputy sheriff (her husband David) to come home from a T-ball game and state that we were going to homeschool seemed like an act of God," she says. "I only committed to doing this for one year, however." The plan was to homeschool for one year, then enroll their son into a parochial school for first grade. Both Christina and David had been raised in Catholic schools and taught by religious brothers and sisters. However, they felt that today's Catholic schools didn't offer the same kind of education for their own children. "We had experienced an innocence of childhood and profound depth for our Catholic faith, which we saw diminishing in Catholic schools," she explains. However, once the year was up, Christina decided to try it for one more year. "I realized there were many positives to homeschooling," she admits, "and they outweighed any negative reasons. We were reaching for positive goals, rather than avoiding problems." The time flew by. "After three years, our way of life was obviously a calling for the family and my vocation," says Christina.

Chapter Fourteen

The couple read quite a few books on the topic and believed those by Dorothy and Raymond Moore had the greatest impact. They thought Cathy Duffy's books were best for finding quality curriculum and the state guidebooks from Christian Home Educators Association were best for the legal aspects.

Christina soon created her own outlook on how homeschooling should be done in her family. "I tried to gear the teaching to Stephen's learning style, making it colorful, musical and organic to the home," she says. "I tried to connect with how he was thinking. As he got older, and his sister Marissa joined us, I realized I was ultimately responsible to God for their religious formation." As she reached that decision, her homeschooling styles began to shift. "I became more organized and let go of some of the spontaneity we had enjoyed in the beginning," she explains. "That was fine with Stephen too. He didn't like a lot of spontaneity. It wasn't his inherent style at all. He liked things written down and organized. Even as a toddler," she chuckles, "he would line up his shoes and toys in perfect order."

The focus of the family's home education was their religion. "Catholic religion classes, rather than the inter-denominational Christian Bible studies, became of paramount importance to my husband and I," she explains. "I am a Catholic revert; I returned to the faith after searching for eight years. I found myself back where I never, ever expected to be and it brought a lot of conflicts." Christina found herself going back and reteaching religious principles to her young children. Much of it was in opposi-

Living His Faith

tion to what they had all learned together in years of weekly Bible study classes. "They asked a lot of questions," she says. "And I had to eat a lot of my words and my fair share of humble pie too."

One characteristic Stephen became known for early on was his singing. "He sang all day long," says Christina. "Everyone knew me as the mom of the kid who sang." When Stephen was nine, his grandmother passed away and it hit him hard. They had had a very close relationship. "He was depressed over it for a long time," says Christina. "He would tell me that he had already accomplished all he wanted to in life and so now he wanted to go to heaven so he could be with Grandma." To help her son heal and capitalize on his drive to sing, Christina enrolled him in the All American Boys Chorus. "When my mom first told me she had put me in the chorus, I screamed NO!" says Stephen. "She had to force me to go. I would only agree to do it for three months." By the time the trial run was over, Stephen was hooked. He stayed with the chorus for seven years and on staff for several more. "I grew to love it," he says. "I ended up making tons of friends during the seven years I sang with them and to this day I see and talk to a good number of guys I sang with." His involvement in chorus led to trips to Canada for four summers in a row, a week in the Midwest and even two weeks in Japan. He performed in concerts, as both part of the choir and as a soloist. As a senior at Thomas Aquinas College, he has been in the college's choir for three years and last year, played the lead role—an archangel—in a musical called "Herrod."

Chapter Fourteen

The years he spent singing were wonderful, but it was his time on the staff as a Prefect of Discipline that made the most impression on him. It was a part time job with full time responsibilities and time requirements, according to Christina. "He really developed a strong character and helped to diffuse problems between other boys." From 9th to 12th grade, Stephen also took religion classes with a norbertine priest. In addition to this, he took classes in public speaking, cooking and sports, had a paper route and sang in a youth choir.

"It really helped me to develop some leadership skills," he says. His future may even lie with the Chorus. "They expect and hope to hire him as Dean of Students when he graduates," says Christina, "but he has not decided yet what career he wants to pursue." Stephen is considering working full time with the chorus to help pay off some debts, but it's obvious that he has something bigger in mind down the road somewhere. "I do love sports," he admits, "and I am the sports director here at the college. However, when I am 80 years old and I look back on my life, I want to say something more than I had a good time. I want to know that during my time here I really contributed." His bachelor's degree in Liberal Arts will help him get any number of different jobs; he is even considering becoming a priest. "He will search for his vocation and career with prayer," says Christina, "and try different job situations."

Living His Faith

At one point, Christina considered putting Stephen into high school. The chamber group at Chorus looked like it was going to be part of the chamber group at a Catholic high school and this way he could continue his friendships and singing for four more years. However, when she presented the option to her husband, his response was, "If it ain't broke, don't fix it." Stephen also said he would rather stay at home through the high school years.

Later, his decision began to waver. "Once Stephen was a sophomore, he began to question his former decision," recalls Christina. "New students were painting a pretty picture of public school. Stephen continued to doubt and thought it might be better for him in a traditional school." Christina and David didn't agree. "My husband and I learned that some high schools did not recognize the work homeschooling students had accomplished and required them to start over at 9th grade," she says. "We could not pay tuition at a Catholic school; financially, it would be a hardship. Stephen just submitted to us quietly."

Like other homeschoolers, Stephen found himself wondering what typical high school activities are like—and if he was missing anything. "I used to think it was a disadvantage that I would not be able to go to high school football games or proms or other school dances," he says. "Well, I actually got to go to prom as a senior, because a friend of mine that went to public school invited me. When I get there, I remember thinking that

Chapter Fourteen

there wasn't really anything so great about it. The place was crowded. People were so physical it looked like they were having sex on the dance floor and the music wasn't that good. That's when I realized that all of my ideas about dances weren't true."

Stephen's transition to college was a slightly bumpy one. "The first year I was pretty homesick," he says. "I know there are a lot of kids out there who are eager to get away from home, but I liked it there. My friends were still back there and I had a good life that I enjoyed." His mother remembers that first semester well. "He may not say this," she says, "but all he did was study the whole time. He never went out and had fun. Never took choir or sports." Stephen agrees. "I was feeling really lonely at first, but my second semester I started to relax and make friends. I learned how to balance things better." Academically, the transition from home-schooling to college wasn't difficult, although he quickly found out that his old skill of being able to just memorize information and then move on didn't work at college. "I came here because I wanted to broaden my mind," he explains. "I wanted to under-stand the deeper meaning in things. I think a lot more actively here and I have found that it is really true that the more you read, the more you exercise your mind."

When Christina looks back on her years of homeschooling Stephen, she says it is easy to see the best part of it—and the hardest. "The best is just being close to my children," she says. "They discuss everything with us to this day. Through homeschooling, I got to see my children grow up day-by-day, enjoy them at all stages of growth and answer God's call to give them a good spiritual foundation." On the other hand, it was a real challenge for her. "The hardest part was

Living His Faith

being a servant to them, no matter how I felt. God stretched me thin to be transparent to my children, faults and all. It is a very humbling experience to admit I am wrong," she says, "that I make mistakes and I don't feel like doing what I am supposed to do. But," she adds, "I would do it all over again."

Stephen's homeschooling and his foundation in his faith have created a man who is on the edge of walking out into the world with a degree in one hand and a great deal of moral strength and conviction in the other. "Because I was home-schooled, I received not only a good education, but also was spiritually formed as well," he says. "This gave me a solid foundation in my faith before I faced the pressures of the world and it is a large part of why I think I still live my faith."

Chapter Fifteen

Michael—A Charmed Life

If a person wanted to play the lottery, they should send Michael to purchase the ticket. "This boy just leads a charmed life," says his mother Kathleen and it's true. One look at what has happened to him in his mere 18 years proves it.

"The first time was when he was about seven years old," says Kathleen. "We had a lot of books and videos," she explains. "Michael knew that we couldn't use them all the time and that other kids might like a chance. So, he built a library in the garage." Michael kept regular hours for two summers in a row, loaning out movies and books complete with cards, pockets and even fines. "The media found out about it," says Kathleen, "and he was put on the front page of the newspaper with color photos." A neighbor sent the story to then First

After Homeschool
Fifteen Homeschoolers Out In The Real World

Chapter Fifteen

Lady Barbara Bush and days later; seven-year-old Michael got a Letter of Commendation from the White House. "That is indicative of his life for the last twelve years," adds Kathleen with a note of pride.

His luck was only starting, however. After going to kindergarten and first grade, Kathleen pulled Michael out of school. Even though Kathleen wanted to homeschool from the first, thanks to hearing about it through La Leche League and attending a conference with the famous Colfax family, her ex-husband wasn't so sure. "It wasn't that he was unsupportive of the idea," she explains. "He just figured that if we were paying more than $10,000 a year in property taxes, we should get something for it! Half-day kindergarten wasn't so bad," she reflects. "Full day first grade was awful. He was gone from 8am until 4pm each day and we were completely tied down to the public school schedule."

Since Michael's parents were both freelance court reporters, they enjoyed the freedom their jobs gave them. With Michael in school, that freedom was limited. "After a while, we didn't even consider anything else than homeschooling," she says. "It was our lifestyle." Both of Michael's brothers, Rafael or "Raffi", 9, and Brandon, 16, were homeschooled from the very start. Kathleen herself played a significant role in homeschooling in her state. She is the president of the state Alliance of Home Education and in the past, she ran the Homeschool Connection, one of the most popular homeschooling law sites on the Internet. "It was tough," she recalls. "I had more than 500 emails every single day." Since then she has done radio shows about homeschooling, as well as testified in court for other homeschooling families.

Michael's family considers themselves to be structured unschoolers—an unusual term. "It really isn't an oxymoron," says Kathleen with a chuckle. "We mixed and matched curriculum, but if we had a chance or an opportunity to go and do something, we went. They need another term for people like us. Opportunistic homeschoolers is what comes to mind." Kathleen also utilized a lot of different tutors for her boys. "We had every-

A Charmed Life

thing from piano teachers and college classes to other home-schooling moms. I teach chemistry and physics to other home-schoolers through our local group," she adds. This isn't just a vol-unteer position; in her group, the moms are paid to teach classes to the homeschoolers. "I took classes with the Adult Ed depart-ment, our local community college, our church, Boy Scouts, other homeschooling mothers, our vo-tech culinary school and other places," says Michael.

During his homeschooling years, Michael was in the Order of the Arrow honor society, worked at a child care Kindermusik studio, did two years at McDonald's and then had a job as line cook at an upscale restaurant for eight months. He took piano les-sons for 14 years, along with a lot of art classes.

When he was 15, Michael's good luck popped up again. "Fifteen Boy Scouts were selected from the entire state," explains Kathleen, "and he was one of them. He went to the Empire State Building and spent the night up there on the Observation Deck. Pizza. Sleepover. Everything." Michael spent eleven years in Boy Scouts and his recent Eagle Scout project, done during his sum-mer break from college, involved carving out heavily wooded sec-tions of a local non-profit campground in order to create new campsites. The whole area was covered in Japanese rose thorn bushes, so the going was slow—and risky.

Working with a landscape architect, Michael organized the cutting down of 47 "junk" trees, removed the stumps and rocks and graded a section so that it could be used for picnic tables. All the poison ivy was taken out and wood chips were brought in. The next complication was getting water to the area—the nearest waterline was 600 feet away. A backhoe was brought in and a trench was dug. PVC pipe was laid and new hydrants were put into place. After that, Michael created 22 wooden signs of varying size. Each one was stained, waterproofed, lettered and painted. Of course, then he had to dig two feet down to install the posts. Finally, he built a retaining wall on the nature trail to replace one

Chapter Fifteen

that had been washed out. A sixty page written report detailing what he did, how many hours he put in (210) and who helped him was turned in, along with about 40 before and after photos. All of the equipment, supplies and services for this project were either donated or paid for through fund raising. The total cost ran approximately $5000. Michael somehow fit this in between the 50 hours a week he was working as a chef.

Cooking became Michael's biggest passion. "When I was 14," he explains, "I took 14 weeks of cooking classes. I was then invited to take a two-year high school class but since I was advanced; I worked as the teacher's assistant. He asked me what I wanted to do next." At 16, he attended a year at the local community college and then his parents "graduated" him from High School homeschooling. "I just wanted all of my sons to find out whatever it was that made them happy," says Kathleen. "I didn't want to tell them what it was. For Michael, it was cooking." He decided to apply to the Culinary Institute of America in Hyde Park, New York.

"I thought, 'What the heck!'" says Michael. "I knew I could never afford it but why not give it a try?" Michael's application was one of 19,000 to a college that has a notoriously low acceptance rate. To no-one's surprise, Michael was selected. He was the youngest student to ever be accepted. Not only that, but he was also awarded a significant scholarship from one of the most prestigious places in the cooking world—the James Beard Foundation. It wasn't the only one either. Michael received scholarships from the National Restaurant Educational Association, the New Jersey Bakers Board of Trade and others.

"We had so many scholarships, we weren't sure what to do," says Kathleen. The first year, Michael had $20,000 worth in multiple scholarships. He was selected as the 2001 Scholarship Recipient for the Top United States Culinary Student and at 16, was knighted into the culinary association, the Confrerie de la Chaine des Rotisseurs. When he gave his acceptance speech for winning the Top Culinary Student of the United States spot, he received a standing ovation. "He was overwhelmed with the

A Charmed Life

recognition that he got," says Kathleen. "He wonders how he could deserve all this when he is just following his own dreams. Of course, I believe he deserves it all. He works so hard and everyone just loves him."

Michael was never the rebellious type of teen that is so often portrayed in the media. "What people don't seem to realize," he says, "is that today's teen is created by the school. The stress, the go—there just isn't a lot of space for all of those egos. In homeschooling there is no issue about fitting in. You always fit in."

One of the things that make Michael's accomplishments so surprising to some is that he is also dyslexic. "I never bothered getting him technically classified," says Kathleen. "I knew what he could and couldn't do and always concentrated on his strengths as he learned to compensate for his weaknesses. I could have tortured this child for 12 years just like the public school would've done if I had left him there, over things like spelling which his brain simply isn't hardwired to do. It never 'clicked'," she continues, "and by 7th grade, I knew it never would. I—or the public school—could have spent his entire childhood convincing him he was stupid and an underachiever. I got him out of there just in time. For anyone to say that public school 'professionals' might have made a significant difference if he had been there," she adds, "I say what naiveté. No one can cure dyslexia. It just is. The most they could hope to do is help each dyslexic learn to cope but there is no standard coping method. It differs from person to person. An aware homeschooling parent, however, doesn't have to pressure his/her child to learn to cope while maintaining self-esteem and confidence. I am so proud of my son, that he can accomplish so much and be so talented and learn to compensate in ways that are simply unique unto himself." Michael is grateful too. "I know I would have been held back academically by being labeled in the public school," he says.

Today, Michael is getting to graduate from college (March 2003) at the young age of 20. "I feel very fortunate," he says. "I have met people here at CIA who have dreamed of coming here all of their lives. I don't want to tell them that I just heard about

After Homeschool
Fifteen Homeschoolers Out In The Real World

Chapter Fifteen

it and a few weeks later, I was accepted." His future plans aren't set in stone yet, but he hopes to travel to Italy, Asia and France and live there for three to four years at a time as a chef. "I don't think that I would ever be here without homeschooling," he says. "It enabled me to have a great freedom to study anything I wanted. I was given the opportunity to discover what I wanted to do with my life without pressure to conform."

Dedicated as he is, Michael also thoroughly enjoys the chance to play. "I am an outdoors, adrenaline, gotta-do-it-now type of guy," he says. To prove it, he has a place on CIA's paintball team. "We play in collegiate tournaments," he says. The grin in his voice is evident as he mentions that he just bought a paintball gun that shoots twenty balls per second.

His mother's predictions of where Michael might end up are vague. "My mind doesn't really get wrapped up around expectations," she says. "From early on, it appeared Michael's interest was in becoming a musician—he's a classical pianist, as all of my boys are—or maybe a chef—or a priest. I figured all three wrapped into one would make a fine man," she chuckles. "Michael leads a charmed life," she adds, "and so anything can happen. Who knows what he will accomplish in the next three years—or twelve! Watching your children far exceed what you thought possible is the best part of homeschooling."

What about Michael's brothers? How do they feel about their older brother who has achieved this much so fast? "They have their own strengths," she says. "Brandon is interested in computer animation or law enforcement and Raffi is as charismatic and personable as they come. He would make a terrific politician!" As for feeling like they are living in their brother's shadow, the boys are accepting. "They know it's a big shadow," says Kathleen, "since Michael is 6'4" and 250 pounds. However, they are all quite loving towards each other, so it isn't a problem."

Brandon's sarcastic comment in the background summed up his thoughts on his popular and lucky older brother. "Oh, wow," he says in a deadpan voice. "Michael was selected to be in a book. I am soooooo surprised."

Chapter Sixteen

Brendan—A Conduit for Grace

When Eileen first heard that a friend of hers was going to homeschool, her first reaction was critical. "I asked her, 'Why do you always have to do everything against the status quo? Are you going to keep your children in a glass cage?'" Soon after that, Eileen discovered not only did she have a growing dissatisfaction with the material being used in the Catholic school her children were enrolled in; she had the same feeling about her faith itself.

The school had brought in a new series of reading books that she and her husband John—along with other parents—objected to. "We were concerned about the heavy occult element in the series," she says. Coupled with the fact that an increasing number of students in the Catholic school were not Catholic at all but just enrolling in order to avoid the area busing, Eileen was upset. "We

Chapter Sixteen

were lukewarm in our faith," says Eileen. "Despite all of my luke-warm-ness," she says, "I heard things like that and began to boil in passion for my faith. I had assumed my kids were getting a good foundation in their Catholic faith, but this episode shocked me into reality." Eileen objected and in doing so, she felt her reputation was on the line. "I felt singled out by the community," she says. "I felt more than a little foolish."

Eileen removed Brendan from school over Easter break. "I had suddenly been woken up to the fact that my husband and I were responsible for teaching our faith to our children and that we had been taking the easy way out," she says. "I also realized that something precious was being taken away—fervent faith—and I wanted it all the more." Eileen spent the summer reading all the books on homeschooling she could find, but felt the greatest source of advice and help was the people she knew who were already homeschooling.

John, her husband, supported the idea, but didn't really play a role in the early years. "He was going through some radical employment changes," says Eileen, "and I didn't want to add to it—at least, not until I was nearly going out of my mind," she says with a grin. "As the kids have grown, he has had a bigger role in making decisions—and he can be the bad guy for a change."

Brendan was not thrilled with the idea at first. "I can't believe how upset I was when my mom announced we were going to homeschool," he recalls. According to Brendan, his distress was because, by only the second grade, he had already become far too peer-dependent. "I was a follower for sure," he says. "I was already following my friends into a sort of organized bullying."

After Homeschool

Fifteen Homeschoolers Out In The Real World

A Conduit for Grace

As the years passed, Brendan's viewpoint of homeschooling has truly matured. "I spent my entire childhood observing the increasing divergence between two paths: the "status quo" path which all of my friends were on and the new radical path I found myself on." His observations on what was happening around him seem to come from hours of thought. "Morally, I saw with horror how the little innocents I knew in second grade were ravaged by the snares of high school and then in comparison, how much of my childhood I was able to retain being at home, instead of always trying to 'grow up' in that never ending pursuit of 'coolness.' On the academic side," he continues, "although both paths remained on roughly the same level, the means to excellence were very different. I never had to deal with the wearisome 'busy work' designed to make sure students understood concepts, because my mom knew exactly what I did and didn't understand. The path I didn't take, along with all of the celebrated rites of passage which are deemed so essential to childhood, did not generally produce men and women, but children wounded and in pain, perhaps wiser for their injuries, but definitely not healthy."

The family followed a rather strict and structured form of homeschooling. Brendan's brothers, Gavin, 19, and James, 13, reacted to it differently. "At first, we enrolled the boys in a home study program," describes Eileen. "That was a great program for Brendan, my more academic child, but it set for a very bad relationship with Gavin. It was far too rigid and stiff for him and it was a catalyst for many battles between us." The program was rather expensive so Eileen began to pick and choose her own curriculum. She filed an affidavit within her county for five years, making their homeschool a private school; later she joined a pub-

Chapter Sixteen

lic charter school for 8th through 12th grades. It was an hour away but it provided a supportive homeschooling community, along with some of the classes her sons would need for graduation. "Speech and Debate taught the boys to think clearly and defend their beliefs powerfully and intelligently," says Eileen. "Athletics were important for physical development and learning to be a team player. Our church youth group provided wholesome entertainment with other Catholic peers and a chance to perform many works of charity and mercy."

Brendan also worked at a local daycare center, summer camp, Pee Wee sports program, sports and Boy Scouts.' They were in the charter school for five years but then the state began to create too much red tape. "It was very, very structured and it felt like someone was hovering over me at all times," says Eileen. "I felt like a real taskmaster because they demanded so much documentation and regular meetings." When her children started turning down great opportunities because their schedules couldn't permit it, Eileen knew something was wrong. "I felt like I was losing my role as teacher with my kids," she says. She left the charter school and went back to their own curriculum. "We returned to learning about our faith, learning Latin and giving a more classical structure to our education," she explains.

In their household, homeschooling was done for a minimum of four hours per day. "We took it all very seriously," says Eileen. All of them had to battle with some degree of burn out. "There were days when it was just drudgery," she admits. "The days of just cleaning the house or meeting a friend or just making snap decisions were gone for me. During the high school years, I made

A Conduit for Grace

the boys pick up their books everyday for academics and put aside other activities. We became less social." They continued to go to church three times a week as well as to monthly confession. Brendan agrees with his mother. "It did become like drudgery," he says. In part, he feels when a person is out in public, he/she gets a shot of adrenaline as he is out around people. "It's like a shot of adrenaline straight into the arm," he says. "When you're at home, you don't get that shot. But, just because something is occasionally not fun, it doesn't mean that the goal is not worthy. The means can be hard but the cause is noble."

"While trying their hardest to make our education fit our particular needs, my parents were also very conscious of the standards of public schools," explains Brendan. "That meant we always did 180 days of school and a certain number of hours units, covering at least the key points of learning in a subject either outlined explicitly or just traditionally upheld. The style wasn't oppressive," he continues. "Even though we had to spend a given amount of hours in a subject, there was a lot of freedom to do what we please with those hours. We might use a textbook during the year as a reference and framework, but I was always allowed to run off after an interesting lead or pour over books from the library and movies and documentaries that pertained to the certain rivulet I happened to be wading in at the time." Brendan says that his mother occasionally had to resort to other methods than 'gentle persuasion' to remind him and his brothers to do what they were supposed to do. "Grounding happened," he says with a smile.

Chapter Sixteen

"The worst part of homeschooling for me," says Eileen, "was always waking up knowing we had to hit the books once again and trying to tell yourself to keep putting one foot in front of another. Demanding that reports and papers be handed in on time and then enforcing it was hard and of course, every teacher's bane is grading." The best part, on the other hand? "Being able to step off the world's rat race and keep a slower pace."

Brendan's perspective on his teenage years is perceptive. "All the problems a teenager goes through, I went through, only perhaps in miniature," he says. "The central conflict of teenage years, the desire to be independent co-existing alongside the need for your parents and a desire to be loved by them, comes out clearly in homeschooling. I wanted so much to control my life, to control my education, to take things into my own hands, that having to submit to the teaching/parental figure in my mom was grating to my pride," he adds. "The underlying theme of all our family meetings was always how to maintain that delicate balance of dependence and independence." There is a solution to all the tension and the angst however. "This is all counteracted by a strong family bond, lots of love and a unity of purpose among the entire family. Parents should never hide their reasons from their children, especially concerning homeschooling, but should frequently discuss why they are doing what they are doing and what goals they hope to obtain. This brings the kids from a state of merely obeying—which often leads to rebellion—to a state of unity with the parents, so that the entire family is one in mind and heart."

A Conduit for Grace

Eileen believes one of the main keys to successfully home-schooling is finding the right support group. "The kids get opportunities for like minded friends and field trips but it is for the mental health of the mom. As the kids are out playing the field," she adds, "the moms are pouring out their souls, frustrations and trials. Right when you are tempted to give it all up, someone lays information in your lap or just whispers a comforting, 'oh that happens in our house too!' and then everything seems all right again. You just have to have a support group or someone to unload on!"

Eileen believes it is especially important that a support group be based in the family's faith, if at all possible. "Even though our Protestant sisters are the pioneers of the movement," she says, "and are doing a spectacular job raising soldiers for Christ, we as Catholics always have to leave out the Virgin Mary in our conversations. Do get to know many moms from all homeschooling groups, but make sure you primarily have Catholic supporters."

Brendan sometimes suffered from a lack of what he called "companions on the road to truth." He felt a lack of friends sometimes, as well as frustration that he couldn't be involved with as many sports as he would have liked to. However, like most home-schoolers, he thinks the supposed lack of socialization myth that haunts the movement is, in his opinion, "hogwash." "Baseball teams, church activities, family functions and neighborhood children all provided ample means for socialization," he says. "In fact, as we tagged along with our mom to different places like city hall,

Chapter Sixteen

elderly homes, grocery stores and just around town, we also got to socialize with people not our own age, something other kids miss out on. This tends to breed contempt for the older generation, causing the youth to miss out on all their elders have to offer. On the other hand," he continues, "we gained the confidence and manners to behave properly around adults, an invaluable skill for the future, and we also got to enjoy the company and friendship of older people we would never have come into contact with otherwise."

"I feel incredibly blessed to have been homeschooled," says Brendan. Although he is not sure what he is going do with his future, it is apparent from talking to him that it will be profound. He is driven by a spiritual desire to share what he calls 'the truth' with others, either through speaking, writing, teaching or a combination of all three. When he tries to articulate just what the truth is, he pauses. "I don't want to sound too mystical here," he says with a smile. He compares it to the images that authors Tolkein and CS Lewis used in their books. "They use myth for those of us who are stuck in the gray, concrete world and they show the beauty and the color behind the curtain. It is a symbol of grace," he adds.

Brendan's viewpoint of the world seems far more in depth than the typical college students. "The meaning of life seems to be missing in people," he says. "It's all about money or power or pleasure and the energy, life and passion seem to be deflating."

A Conduit for Grace

Eileen thinks her son will eventually become either a college professor or a priest, but Brendan is not sure. He is truly torn between two polar opposite life directions. On the one hand, he wants to be a priest. "A priest in the pulpit has always attracted me," he says. "I want to be a conduit of grace to inspire people's hearts. I want to lead them through the tributaries to the great river." On the other hand, he is equally driven to become both a husband and a father. "The family is a reflection of the Trinity," he explains. "I love children so very much and I want to teach, lead and produce good warriors for the faith." The passion Brendan has for his faith and the meaning of life is in every word he speaks. It is also there when he speaks of the young lady he has been courting for the last year. "We took two years to grow and develop a very special friendship first," he says. "A year ago, we decided to take it to the next step and our relationship is both profound and amazing."

"We are so very proud of Brendan," says Eileen. "He has gone way beyond what we expected. He is really striving to be a man and through the grace of God, he is a true homeschooling success." Brendan aspires in everything he does to meet his college's motto of The Good, the True, the Beautiful. "All of those are contained in or are actually God," he says. "I see the path I took as one leading naturally to manhood, I had my father to learn from, I had the protective and corrective influence of my family and I had the inspiration and aid of the Faith."

Essay

Homeschooling Vibrato

by Ben Kniaz

(reprinted with permission by the author and Home Education Magazine)

Last fall, I transferred as a sophomore to the Thomas More College of Liberal Arts in New Hampshire. Its tiny colonial campus and double-digit student body lend the college an air of secret value. And it is a jewel, although the academic pressure runs high. Often I and others have to escape the atmosphere in my oh-so-popular car. At the end of the first month, when the excitement of being in a new place has been replaced by the realities of a full semester ahead—I remember getting into my Nissan one day with tall, easy-going Dan and smoky, taciturn Rueben.

Homeschooling Vibrato

Autumn air lifted our spirits as I drove us to the Merrimac Public Library. We were members of "the band", a group of guys who were beginning to meet about once a week to bank on the piano and try out tunes some of us had written. For knowing these two so little, I was already beginning to feel quite fond of them both. Playing music together does that. Dan is 23, loves cooking and worked as a youth minister for a church before deciding to go back to school. Rueben is 24. After high school, he lived with his grandparents in South Korea for a year, where he decided to return to the States and attend a small, serious university. He has been writing music for at least eight years now, mostly for himself. The music that we played that semester has come to embody, for me, the unaffected, unfinished people and character of our band. Listening to our music, I sense the spontaneous creativity—too rough around the edges to be sold—that I so love about the homeschooling way of life.

Music is so fragile—one note missed and the whole thing can fall apart. I recognized this most clearly when I played violin in a classical senior high orchestra and lived in fear of playing into that moment of silence in the music. But when the most self-confident music (rock, rap, etc.) is deeply insecure; if the drummer hiccups, suddenly the whole thing begins to sound like country (well… if you stretch your imagination!). The instruments playing the music share this fragility, as well. My violin rests infant-like under my chin, as if waiting for the day it will be smashed. Our lives can seem no less precarious.

After Homeschool
Fifteen Homeschoolers Out In The Real World

by Ben Kniaz

Yet it is just at the moment when a classical composer rests the relative strength of the symphony orchestra on one instrument, just when that cello reaches out by itself over an entire orchestra to play its solo that I am struck by the beauty of the music and its composer. The fragility is touched when that inner string is touched and quivers in unbearable weakness; and the strength and brilliance gained by such weakness comes to light. For this reason, I have always (unconsciously) felt that the best music is also the music that trusts its fragility most.

Reading the greek tragedies and comedies at Thomas More College, I noticed that my classmates were particularly enthralled by Aeschylus' Prometheus Bound. In their papers, they tried to understand Prometheus' gift of blind hope to man: the gift to not foresee coming doom. I came away with the impression that blind hope is that capability of man to look past the fact that he could die in three seconds and will definitely die sometime in the next 90 years. In our gloomier moments, we do find ourselves crying out, "Vanity, vanity, all is vanity!" For the most part, however, we are blind or wise enough to hope in the life we have. This makes it possible and enjoyable to continue caring and creating. And this is what I sense in the weakness of music: music is the radiant outcome of blind hope. It tangibly speaks our 'breakability' and it makes that fragility completely endearing.

Homeschooling Vibrato

While listening to Bach, one gets the impression that he deeply felt the sweet delicacy of life. His music encircles the courtyard of the human heart behind shadowy marble columns. It always maintains an ordered passion and privacy. I well imagine that fragility of Bach's culture in his music—its trust in court formality and grace. A culture can be as breakable and endearing as music. My gut feeling is that the same is true about homeschooling.

As a homeschool graduate looking back, I appreciate that my schooling experience was a way of life, not simply a way of education. It was me at 14 sitting at the computer planning an entire 3D computer game that I was going to design on my own, while the school kids memorized facts in history class. It was me playing an enjoyable game of baseball with other homeschoolers two feet shorter and seven years younger than me, painfully sensible all the time at how silly I must look to the outside world. It was me walking into a classroom at the public high school to take the SATs and physically comprehending that I didn't belong in that life, academic or social. But, returning from some social activity or soccer practice, it crossed my mind more than once whether I could belong—or worse—whether I should . . . It was being so at home at home. I would get my math done, eat pasta for lunch, and then find the day melting into the penetrating voice of a toddler, the dog barking when my dad came home, the dinner and dish washing, the sound of crickets and the essay I sketched out until two in the morning. My homeschooling experience was me prac-

by Ben Kniaz

ticing a violin concerto while wandering around the house in growing fear of "forever-having-failed" at an upcoming recital. It was cherishing the comment of an old woman who told me afterwards: "You played like a true violinist", *not* "You played without missing a note." It was me sitting at the dinner table with the whole family and talking about *The Lord of the Rings* long before the current hype.

There is something about my schooling years that brings to mind "the band" of last fall. I think it is that the band, like homeschooling, appears most fragile in my memory at exactly the time when it was the most worthwhile to me. We always had more 'important' things we should have been doing with the time we spent jamming (such as, say, preparing for the test the next morning!) Several times, the less benevolent upperclassmen told us to stop because we were playing too loud for their studying. We didn't have the organization or the skill to make it big. Some days Dan and I would play Pachelbel's Canon In D, over and over again on piano and violin, aware that it met our moods. And some days, Rueben would bring in his electric guitar and drown us out, as loud as we played, as he built up the power of a song. Once in a while, someone would come up from downstairs in the cafeteria and ask: "Was that really you guys playing right now?" When I replay the tape recordings I made of us, the sound comes out very rough, but also aesthetically subtle. For me, those were the hours when it became clear again why I was spending seven to nine hours a day studying and in class. That inner string was touched.

Homeschooling Vibrato

My 14-year-old brother and I played Frisbee with my five year old sister last evening. After each throw, she ran over to where her apple lay on my brother's jacket to take a bite, which slowed the game down more than a little. But, to the gratification of us all, she began throwing and catching like a real pro in an hour, even running after her own throws when we didn't. Watching her learn to play "like her brothers" is like listening to Bach. It somehow combines with my homeschooling history and the "the band" of last fall to strengthen my conviction that when we hear clear music playing soundtrack in our lives, we should take heart and learn to trust ever more in the fragility of our position.

(A homeschooler most of his life, Ben Kniaz spent the last three years attending four universities—two as a dual-enrollment student. He hopes to stay put the next two years. Ben runs and contributes to www.apricotpie.com, an active site for the writing and musings of homeschooling students.)

Essay

But What About Socialization? The College Test

by Peter Kowalke

I wasn't even paying attention to the first signs proving I had avoided a life of disappointment. There probably were great exhalations of relief from my parents when I started to read at the age of ten, but I was oblivious to the concern, the tense expectation that homeschooling would work, that learning to read would manifest itself in me when the time was right. Only later, in my teen years, did I start to inherit uncertainty that I might be making a mistake by staying away from the classroom. Certainly I cannot speak for every child or teen that doesn't go to school. Drawing from my own experience as a lifelong unschooler (until going to college), as well as my many homeschooling/unschooling friends, I can nonetheless state that not going to school instills at least a modicum of doubt in one's own educational choices.

But What About Socialization?

Am I going to learn as much as my peers in school? Am I going to have problems with socialization? Will there be unforeseen difficulties in my life as a result of not attending grade school, middle school or even high school? Will I be able to get into college and reach my potential? Will employers want to hire me?

To this point, I keep breathing sighs of relief; I'm no dullard, homeschooling hasn't blindsided me with any deleterious effects (yet?), I'm halfway through my college experience and don't have a problem making friends or acquaintances. I'm still uncertain about the final hurdle that unschooling must pass—my ability to acquire a worthwhile job but so far so good. Before I resume my incessant worry about finding a good job, however, let's take a look back at the common homeschooling concern of socialization and pay attention to social life during my first year out of the house and away at Hampshire College.

Moving out of my secluded house in the woods and into a dorm that was surrounded by over 58,000 students of approximately the same age (the combined total of Smith, Amherst, Mount Holyoke and Hampshire colleges, as well as the University of Massachusetts), I didn't quite know what to expect. Accustomed to meeting new acquaintances irregularly, I was conditioned to making friends easily and spending time with said friends whenever possible. However, 58,000 potential friends, all readily accessible, made me fear that my lack of the social indifference my peers had formed during a lifetime of schooling might cause conflict with other activities in my life, namely academics. Although it could be reasonably assumed that I wouldn't be tempted by parties and college vices such as alcohol, smoking or drugs, what if I socialized to my heart's content and didn't ever study? Not having experience being around so many kids on a daily basis, there were no guarantees that I would stay as focused in college as when I was studying and working at home.

After Homeschool
Fifteen Homeschoolers Out In The Real World

by Peter Kowalke

During the first few weeks of class, my fears almost looked justified; I was a social maven. Now I'm not intimating that I was Mr Popular; there were other people magnets drawing attention and affection from everyone. I could only marvel and take notes from the social mastery of such individuals. Donning my own, patented brand of charisma as amiability and courage to freely introduce myself to strangers, I might consider myself well known, if not exactly 'popular'. In my first few weeks at Hampshire, I would frequent certain halls every evening, catch movies with new friends, attend guest lectures and play cards with hall-mates. My academics didn't suffer much, but in retrospect I probably should have studied more.

Spending copious amounts of my day making friends and feasting on the social buffet I had never known as an unschooler (apart from my yearly pilgrimage to the homeschooling conference hosted by the Clonlara School), my academics were saved only by the fact that workloads start gently and gather steam as the semester progresses. In the first few weeks of class, most new Hampshire students—myself included—were finding their social identity and starting to build the core of their social existence while away at college.

By the fourth week, most students had chosen their social orbits and had begun to revolve around the same group of friends, whereas I was still cheerfully making new acquaintances and consciously avoiding favoritism. I limited myself to the people of Hampshire's campus, population of about 1,100, but that still left a lot of introductions. Every meal, I would try to sit at a table with at least one person I had never met and one with whom I was already acquainted. In my mind it was a solid strategy, building both new and existing friendships.

But What About Socialization?

Sitting down with me during lunch at the dining commons would quell the concerns of any homeschooling parent worried about their child's ability to socialize; outgoing, jovial, empathic, laughing with friends I had only recently met, I was the spitting image of good social habits. Socialization? Ha—unschoolers are great at social situations!

Social 'situations' may have been a strong suit, but social experience was another story. Once my fellow students and I realized that we had to hit the books and get to the business of academic education, each student embarked on his or her own time-tested strategy for balancing the social with the academic. The campus quickly slipped into study mode and it was at that point that many of my friends started to relegate themselves to certain social groups. For much of my first semester, I could not fathom why anyone would want to limit their social circle; I kept making new friends and boarding the different social circles, dividing myself equally among all.

Although steadfast in my conviction that I was good at socializing, that homeschooling had not left me an introverted teenager with perverse social habits (after all, I had been to four proms!), frustration began to mount when professors started to dole out homework and assignments; I was suddenly left without time for people interaction while others seemed to maintain a solid balance. Hampshire being a selective liberal arts institution, I was surrounded by valedictorian and intelligent folk, all of whom seemed to have mastered the art of finding time for recreation and movies while concurrently zipping through their studies. I, on the other hand, could rarely find time for a movie. I certainly couldn't give the time necessary for deep, emotionally satisfying friendships. As a result of my inexperience with the social dynamics of institutional education, a lot of people knew my name but none would probably include me in their inner circle, include me as anything more than an acquaintance.

After Homeschool
Fifteen Homeschoolers Out In The Real World

by Peter Kowalke

Being just an 'acquaintance' harbored severe doubt in my social skills. Were homeschooling critics correct when they proclaimed that a life away from school translated into a socially hampered existence full of disappointment? I was 19, living in a tiny cubicle of a room and had no friends, no prospects for romance, no emotional support, no camaraderie beyond the superfluous, fluffy façade of friendly conversation after class or at the dinner table. Worse, it appeared there wasn't even time in my life to build a strong bond with another person.

The first semester at Hampshire College was rough. More than just socially inexperienced at the art of balancing friends and class time, I was seen as an oddity; I smiled too broadly, showed too much interest, appeared too happy, didn't confine myself to a particular social group. Students didn't avoid or ostracize me. After all, we were at a school without grades, tests or majors (pretty liberal). Still, the combination of lacking good friends and being different, even when difference was celebrated (although still labeled 'different'), was enough to re-instill long-forgotten doubt about my ability to integrate with 'school kids.'

Doubt didn't last the year, fortunately. A liberal arts education is supposed to enhance my ability to think critically and instill an awareness of the world around me. It is also, to quote Mary Brown Bullock of Atlanta's Agnes Scott College, supposed to give "the knowledge and thinking skills that transcend a particular discipline or time frame" and allow me to adapt to new situations and jobs of any flavor. In a related vein, it strikes me that unschooling has given me a general foundation for life and social interaction. I may be inexperienced at the art of cultivating deep friendships and I may rely too heavily on an idealized conception of reality, forgetting that people can be mean and innocent behavior can sometimes be construed as malicious intent. That doesn't imply a lack of ability, however and it also doesn't mean that I'll wander the streets of life unequipped to be a social citizen. I just

But What About Socialization?

need to adjust to a new system of social interaction, in this case one that many have already learned.

Returning from winter break, I met a girl named Tina. She was originally from China—had moved to the United States at the age of six. Tina introduced me to her close friend, Andria, an international student from Cyprus. A few days later, the two girls took me out to eat for my birthday. Appreciating the gesture and thoroughly impressed, I suspended my usual habit of frequenting many tables at mealtime and, whenever possible, made a point to sit with both Tina and Andria. A friendship was cultivated, strengthened as I met and made friends with their tiny group of pre-existing friends.

The more time spent with Tina and Andria, the less was available for other social interaction. Despite a continued acquaintance with those I had already met and a persistent desire to meet new people, nearly all spare time was channeled into my newfound group, be it in the form of study sessions or recreation. I stopped sitting at other tables and the growth of my social circle slowed, which was alarming. Concern faded, though, when I realized that my social life had not disintegrated. To the contrary, I now had a healthy social life, full of interrelated friendships, a plethora of acquaintances and two or three really close friends, those with whom I could laugh and share, those I could cherish.

Although I still have a distinctive style that often sets me apart in a crowd and sometimes I must adapt to social interaction that others consider basic, unschooling has not killed my social life. If anything, I'd like to believe that unschooling has aided my interaction with others. I'm not jaded and pessimistic about friendship, suspicious of others or shy about letting my true colors fly. As I once told an acquaintance, I'll make friends with anyone who will let me be their friend.

After Homeschool
Fifteen Homeschoolers Out In The Real World

by Peter Kowalke

*Peter Kowalke, now 24, is a producer and journalist based near Cleveland, Ohio. Married to Mae Rose Shell, also a lifelong unschooler, Peter's written more than two dozen articles about the homeschooling experience. His most significant homeschooling work to date has been **Grown Without Schooling**, a 107 minute documentary he released in 2002. The documentary follows 10 grown homeschoolers, ranging in age from 19 to 31, as they explore and candidly discuss the lasting influence of home education. You can purchase a copy of **Grown Without Schooling**, and help support Peter's future creative works in the process, by sending a check or money order for $24.95, payable to Peter Kowalke, to the Grown Without Schooling documentary, P.O. Box 772, Mentor, Ohio 44061. More information and a video preview are available at www.GrownWithoutSchooling.com. Peter can be reached at peter@kowalke.info or through his personal web site, PeterKowalke.com. He's still a friend to all he meets!*

Epilogue

Ponderings On The Future

Every single one of the profiles included in this book shows the myriad ways that families can homeschool. Each young adult and his family had different inspirations for choosing homeschooling, different ways of doing it, different directions to follow and vastly different results—and therein lies the profoundly special thing about homeschooling. Instead of everyone being thrown into the same environment, the same classes, the same expectations and the same ages, homeschooling families have room for intense individuality. They have space where their children—their unique, diverse, special, one of a kind children—can become who they were intended to be—not what the school, the teachers or the peers pressured them to be. It gives them the freedom to be different, to not learn things the same way as all the other 8 year-olds or 13 year-olds but when, where and how they need to learn it. It allows a chance for each person to decide what works and what doesn't. What fits and what doesn't. What needs extra effort and what doesn't.

Epilogue

How will this affect them as they enter this so-called real world? How will these young adults be different with years of learning who they are and what they want from life? How will it effect them if they know from years of studying and learning without daily coercion and threat of punishment (i.e. low grades and their repercussions) that motivation and success come from within, not from without?

I cannot help but believe that they will make the world a richer, more unique place with their individuality. I am excited and eager to see what this new generation brings. I want to continue to research, read the stories, hear the statistics and listen to the studies. I want to sit down and talk to these young adults, each and every one of them, and find out where they came from and where they are going. Interviewing the fifteen here was an adventure for me. The huge range of opinions and backgrounds, the obstacles and the aspirations, the huge differences in journeys was fascinating and educational.

Meeting these young people also helped me on my own personal road as a homeschooling mother. One of the harder lessons that I have had to learn is to not only hope for others to accept our family's differences but to learn to respect my own children's differences. I remember my parents' faces when they learned I was going to homeschool. Shock, surprise and yes, most likely disappointment. They'd just spent thousands of dollars and four years on my college education in which I had gotten a degree to become a teacher, for goodness' sake, and here I was bucking the entire system with my own children. Thankfully, they respected my decision even as they disagreed with it. That was more of a lesson for me than I had ever anticipated. I quickly came to realize one of the hardest facts about homeschooling: raising a child to be an individual means accepting it when he/she chooses to express individuality. Like many other things in life, easier said than done.

Ponderings On The Future

As my oldest approached that magic age of 18, as she calls it in her essay, she began to increasingly do things that felt uncomfortable for me—or, in other words, not the way I was used to or would have chosen for her. She wore clothes that I detested. She took a lovely shirt I had just given her, cut it up along the seams, took off the sleeves and then fastened the sides back up with safety pins. Gone were the clothes that had any relationship to femininity, replaced with black and burgundy baggy pants and oversized sweatshirts that completely obscured my beautiful daughter. The nerve of this child to dress in clothes that she choose instead of the ones I would have selected for her. Was it necessary that she have a mind of her own in absolutely everything?!

Then along came the boyfriend. Fortunately, both my husband and I really like him—but neither of us are remotely ready for him to be our son-in-law. We're not ready for anyone to be our son-in-law. When she called to tell me about their engagement, I had another hands on, on the job lesson on accepting her individuality. She proposed to him; She gave him the ring. What?! I could feel the words, "That isn't how it's done," rise to my lips, only to be quickly swallowed before they could come out. Instead I found myself uttering the exact same, "oh" that my mother makes when I tell her that I've done something that doesn't fit the mainstream. I tried to summon up as much enthusiasm as possible.

I listened a lot and cried a little and then did what all parents do when their children announce they have chosen a mate: wish or pray it's the right choice. Wish for long lasting happiness and friendship together. Wish they would wait a couple years (at least) before moving from engagement to marriage. Wish for wisdom in your thoughts and words. Wish for the right attitude when it goes wrong or when it goes right. Wish for just a touch of temporary clairvoyance so you know what to prepare for down the road. Mostly I just find myself wishing for a life remote-control device that I can use to push Rewind and go back to where

Epilogue

she is only about six years old again and spend all of those years with her one more time before I surrender her to that real world. Or maybe I could push Fast Forward quickly so I can make sure she is happy in the future and have a little more peace of mind now. Instead I satisfy myself with realizing that my husband and I have brought a wonderful individual into the world to change things and make an impact. Who she does it with and how she does it, no one knows yet. But we will be here for whatever it is.

Homeschooling truly gives parents a stronger chance to raise an individual; a person capable of making decisions, standing on his/her own and choosing life pathways—even if those pathways are not necessarily the one mom or dad perceives as the best one. As can be seen in each of the diverse individuals throughout this book, these young adults are a wondrous and remarkable addition to the world and one that many people—including myself—will be watching with fascination.

A Statement from Thomas Aquinas College
by Jon Daly and Tom Susanka (Admissions)

(A statement from this small college was included because it has such a surprisingly high percentage of homeschoolers. I thought it would be most interesting to find out their thoughts and observations on this new generation coming into their school. In August of 2002, total enrollment was 330—and a full third of them were homeschoolers. —T.O.)

The College Admissions Office at Thomas Aquinas College focuses much of its resources—and plenty of its energy—on recruiting home educated students! Not all of the one hundred home educated students currently enrolled have been home-schooled from kindergarten through 12th grade. About 80 to 85 have done at least the last two years of high school coursework at home. With few exceptions, the College has found home education to have a salutary effect on any student.

Parents who educate their children at home are, we believe, strongly attracted to the curricula and community life of Thomas Aquinas College. The emphasis we place on seeking and living by the truth in all matters has often been mentioned by homeschooling parents as a continuation of their own efforts.

Our experience, over the years, has amply justified early expectations that home educated students would be well-suited to Thomas Aquinas and that they would be successful in its intellectual, spiritual and social life. Freshman begin their studies here looking forward to three things:

(1) a single, non-major and non-elective curriculum which promises them critical judgment in every essential art and science;

(2) direct access to the original works of the foremost philosophers, theologians, scientists, mathematicians and literary figures of the last 2,500 years of western civilization and

(3) vigorous dialogue with classmates and professors—inside and outside of class—concerning the truth of the ideas presented in the 'Great Books' of these authors.

After Homeschool
Fifteen Homeschoolers Out In The Real World

Reading, understanding and profiting from great books doesn't require genius. Good academic preparation does however help! We have found our homeschooled students well prepared for reading and discussing the Great Books. Just as important, they're ready for independent thinking. In seminars and tutorials where analysis, conversation and evaluation replace lectures and note taking, homeschoolers can shine. They have already learned how to learn on their own. This bears fruit when they are asked to develop and articulate their own thoughts in the classroom.

Outside of the classroom, homeschoolers fit in well too. There is, first and foremost, a camaraderie among all students arising from their participation in the one curriculum offered by the College and from the common search for truth and wisdom engendered by great texts and great conversations. A friendly, spirited camaraderie carries over from classrooms to the dining room, commons, dormitories and athletic fields. It is firmly supported by charity and religion. Homeschoolers have come to the College from families where concern for civility, charity and religion are among the very reasons for the truly radical decision to homeschool.

Regarding the admission policy for homeschoolers, the Admission Committee evaluates all applicants, whether home educated or not, for evidence of sufficient ability and preparation for the entire curricula (again, all subjects are studied by all students) and for a good understanding of the unique approach to education taken by the College. Like all applicants, a home education student's application includes:

(1) essay responses to questions posed in the application;
(2) transcripts of high school studies and of any college-level studies undertaken prior to attending Thomas Aquinas College;
(3) three reference letters (one written by a primary teacher and another by another recent teacher, if at all possible; when the parent has been the only teacher, the requirement for a letter from a second teacher is waived) and
(4) SAT I or ACT scores.

We've found home educated students to be beautifully prepared to take their part in this community of young scholars. We welcome and esteem them.

Essay

Homeschoolers and College:
A First Hand Exploration

by Anna Peak

As a kid, I was a little hazy on things like grade-levels, but I always assumed that I, of course, would go to college. Everyone else did, right? And maybe I wasn't really in 'sixth-grade' as a six-year-old, as I briefly thought until speedily disillusioned, however I certainly wasn't going to let anyone get ahead of me. College it would be, then.

I didn't really think about the matter seriously, though, until I was almost sixteen. I was still hazy (despite years of repeated explanations) about the whole grade-level thing, but I figured I was probably ready for college. My first thought, as usual when I wanted to find out about something, was to look for a book on the subject. We had a few thousand books knocking around the house, but few on homeschooling. Most of them mentioned college and at first, what they said seemed reassuring. Some stated, sure, homeschoolers can go to college, and left it at that. I wanted something less vague. Others relied on name-tossing: "Why, homeschoolers can go to Harvard," was a frequent proclamation. Something told me that admission to Harvard was not a guarantee, for homeschoolers or anyone else. Still others made their

Homeschoolers and College

point by way of anecdotes. I remember being particularly appalled to read about a young man who finally managed to persuade Cornell to admit him (with a scholarship covering tuition, room, and board, no less); by the age of sixteen, he was, if I recall correctly, a world-renowned expert on birds who had been invited to give a lecture by the National Audubon Society. In fact, the more I thought about it, the less it seemed I had to go on and the less it seemed I had to offer. But perhaps, I thought, the answers to my questions about college would be found in books on college, not homeschooling.

In those days, I had a library card for public libraries throughout seven different counties, and I went to the college sections of each one and read everything I could find. There were books on the application process (filled with a bewildering array of acronyms), on interviews, on essay-writing, on test preparation, choosing a college, financial aid, scholarships—you name it, I read it. There was a great deal of advice about myriad nuances of the whole process, but I sorted it down to the basics. The SAT was basic. The PSAT (once I learned that a scholarship was possible) was basic. Teacher recommendations and transcripts (I didn't even know what they were at first) were basic. Apparently, to take tests (at least the PSAT) you had to go through your school. To get a transcript and a teacher recommendation, you had to be in a school. I could read about the relative rankings of the schools in the Ivy League and how to reduce my family's EFC on the financial aid forms all I wanted; without being in a school, it seemed I would never get far enough for those considerations to take on any reality.

However, other homeschoolers had gotten into college somehow, and I had to go; I was planning on being a librarian at that point, and a degree was of the essence. There had to be some way around these obstacles. I compared test prep manuals while my mother crossed the first hurdle for me by calling local Christian schools until she found one willing to let me take the PSAT. The Educational Testing Service, it turned out, actually had a school

After Homeschool
Fifteen Homeschoolers Out In The Real World

by Anna Peak

code for homeschoolers, so clearly taking the SAT was possible as well. It seemed that the only special problems left were those of the transcript and teacher recommendation. I decided to let them slide for the moment.

I threw myself into reading guidebooks and ordering catalogues, as well as reading other books. Due primarily to my own self-doubts, I literally studied from morning till night, with only the occasional break—no summer or weekend vacations, and Christmas-tide my only holiday. Reading about college's requirements for non-home-schoolers was disheartening in the extreme—they wanted so many years of math, so many of science, and so on, and really all I'd done was lounge around reading Victorian novels. I was frantic that even if I could convince a college to consider me for admission, I'd be reject-ed because my unstructured education (completely self-taught since age twelve) would be judged worthless. If more information had been available or if I'd had any idea how my reading as an unschooler would allow me to eventually coast through many college classes, my doubts would've disappeared. There just wasn't enough material avail-able on the subject then and unfortunately, colleges weren't exactly falling over themselves to recruit me. I couldn't help but feel that per-haps I deserved it. Surely they knew what they were doing.

Taking the GED (then required in order to be eligible for fed-eral financial aid) helped lay some of those doubts to rest. Quite simply, there is no more egregiously simple-minded test in exis-tence. The test is so easy that (although it is routinely failed by a third of the sample of high-school seniors to whom it's given every year) many homeschoolers have taken and passed it at ages 12 and 13. Accordingly, laws were put in place forbidding anyone younger than 16 to take the test (17 or 18 in some states). As a Michigan resident, I was able to take the test at 16, but I couldn't receive my GED certificate until I turned 18. Thus I technically grad-uated high school a few weeks into my freshman year of college.

By fall of my 'senior year of high school,' I had a list of col-leges I was interested in, good PSAT, SAT, and GED scores behind me, and an impressive reading list. Now it was time to talk to my

Homeschoolers and College

colleges and see what they would require me to do to apply. I soon learned I should've done so long before. Every college I called was happy to have a prospective student on their hands—until they learned I was homeschooled. Some were willing to overlook that, provided that I took a battery of SAT II subject tests or that my SATs were a hundred or two hundred points above their average (and, in the case of Wofford College, a maturity appreciably greater than that of their average student), or some combination of the above. As it happened, my SATs were a few hundred points above the averages of all these colleges (thanks to The Princeton Review's book), but that wasn't the point.

Furthermore, most of the colleges wanted some kind of transcript from me. Even those who had dealt with homeschoolers before didn't seem to understand that a transcript really wasn't possible. When I told them that I had no records, that I had taken no courses, they were bewildered. Having read little about homeschooling, I wasn't able to explain the difference between homeschooling and unschooling, and it probably wouldn't have made much difference anyway; as soon as a college found out that I had taught myself, they were incredulous or downright hostile. When, for instance, I spoke with the director of admissions at my first-choice college, Grove City, he told me (after hearing that I had a 1370) that many people with high scores on the SAT were stupid. He stated that I would have to submit a detailed 'transcript' and various sorts of documentation, along with a letter from someone not involved with education (but still, somehow, knowing all about it) who could attest to my honesty, because 'homeschoolers often lie.' (I should add that Grove City now has a different director of admission, and their policy now seems perfectly reasonable.)

In short, the whole process was rather painful. I took the college catalogues I'd pored over and threw them away, making sure to rip up and spit on the materials sent me from my erstwhile first-choice. My list of colleges had dwindled to nothing, with one notable exception: Hillsdale College, which had never failed to treat me with courtesy. When I spoke with the director of admissions, he not only spelled out what I would have to do to apply

After Homeschool
Fifteen Homeschoolers Out In The Real World

by Anna Peak

(write a description of my studies in lieu of a transcript and have a parent write the teacher recommendation), he talked with me about college homeschool admissions policies in general and how they compared to Hillsdale's (badly), revealing both his eagerness to attract a homeschooler and his knowledge of the subject. That conversation—the man's obvious striving to put me at my ease as much as anything—put the heart back in me. Unfortunately, on reflection, I realized the year I'd planned on going to college had arrived, and I had only one place to apply to, and no guarantee of admission. Even worse, Hillsdale refuses to participate in federal financial aid programs, believing such aid opens the college up to federal control, and my family couldn't afford to pay for my education. I needed all the federal aid I could get, and a scholarship on top of that, or I couldn't go to college.

I returned to researching in earnest. I ordered catalogues wildly, used my father's computer at work to surf the web and re-evaluated my criteria. I had earlier bypassed all women's colleges, fearing that they would be bastions either of raging femi-nazism or southern-belle-ism, but at this point I was desperate. I began to read about single-sex education, and found it had a lot going for it—study after study showed that graduates of women's colleges were more likely to get advanced degrees, more likely to be successful in general, even more likely to marry. I wasn't sure if all that was really true, but clearly these women's colleges must believe it. Surely they must understand what it was to take an unconventional educational path for the sake of principles.

I called every woman's college within an 800 or so mile radius of my home, and almost without exception I met with friendly, even welcoming responses. Mary Baldwin College actually called back to offer me an $8,500 scholarship. I thought that there must be some mistake and pointed out to the woman on the phone that I had no grades, no transcript, just SATs. "Oh, that's fine," she said. "And, just so you know, we'll put it in writing" (a promise she kept). Chestnut Hill College, too, offered me a scholarship of $10,000, again, even before applying. The director of admissions at Rosemont College told me in the course of our

Homeschoolers and College

phone conversation, "I want you to apply." She offered to waive the admissions fee (an offer she honored) and to pay $100 of my travel expenses for me to come visit the campus (I declined—her attitude was enough to convince me I liked the place).

Suddenly I was courted. Things began to fall into place. Surfing the web one day I found the site of Thomas Aquinas College, a small coed college with a Great Books curriculum, which contained an explicit welcome of homeschoolers. I discovered that colleges with similarly unconventional curriculums such as Thomas More and St. John's were also willing to consider my application on a par with anyone. I began to look for colleges that were unusual in any way—Richmond University in London, for instance. The young man I talked to in charge of US recruitment seemed to have no idea what I was talking about, but nevertheless encouraged me to apply. An international perspective, it appeared, made GPAs and SATs seem a lot less like absolute measures of worth and lot more like the relative standards of comparison that they are.

I had plenty of options, at last. I applied to Hillsdale, Mary Baldwin, Chestnut Hill, and Rosemont, and was accepted to each. All required simply that I write up a description of my studies in lieu of a transcript; Hillsdale, as mentioned above, counted a recommendation from my mother as a teacher recommendation, and the others simply asked for recommendations from people who knew me. A few short months later, I was a member of the class of 2002 at Rosemont College, which not only accepted me, but also offered me their highest scholarship, the Cornelian, worth full tuition, despite the fact that I clearly didn't have the 3.7 GPA that was ordinarily one of the requirements. The financial aid package they offered on top of that was generous as well, and a woman from the financial aid office called to let me know that my room and board as well as tuition were covered; the FedEx package confirming that was on its way, just so I would have a day's less worry.

After Homeschool
Fifteen Homeschoolers Out In The Real World

by Anna Peak

My next four years at Rosemont lived up to the promise of those initial encounters. I loved college. Some homeschoolers and particularly unschoolers are deeply suspicious of the whole concept of college, but I saw nothing to complain about. I had a good deal of freedom in choosing courses—a feature not prominent in elementary and high schools, and an important qualitative difference. True, I was often made to do things I'd never willingly have done—read Ovid and Theocritus, for example—they (usually) turned out to be worthwhile. Then again, I was in effect being paid—via my scholarship—to read and write. It certainly beat being paid (considerably less) to bag groceries or file paperwork, and without taking this 'job' I would've been cut off from every career I ever seriously considered—nurse, librarian, professor.

I soon found, too, that I still had enough time for my own activities. Sophomore year found me teaching myself HTML. My first web site, devoted to old radio shows such as *The Shadow*, was so fascinating to make and looked so 'real' that I cast about for ideas for a second site. I saw no point in cluttering the web with yet another Beatles fan page; I wanted to come up with something original on a subject that I could talk with authority: homeschooling and college, of course.

My first concern was to do some research and see if this kind of information didn't already exist. I quickly found that in just a few years things had indeed changed. The GED, for instance, was no longer a requirement for federal financial aid. The list of colleges that have accepted homeschoolers on the "School is Dead—Learn in Freedom" site seemed to contain nearly every college in the country. There were even sites and books and sections of books, I now found, devoted specifically to giving advice to homeschoolers and (if not more so) to their parents on exactly how to apply to colleges. However, all this advice was geared towards more structured homeschoolers, as was clear from the detailed advice many authors gave on how to craft a transcript. A relaxed homeschooler such as I had been would have both a prac-

Homeschoolers and College

tical and an ethical dilemma in crafting such a 'transcript.' Nor did any of these sources provide me with what I had found to be the most crucial information: what does this college or that, specifically, require of homeschoolers? Of course, a homeschooler could just ask. But to make inquiries of many colleges systematically would take a great deal of time, and to only make inquiries of colleges the student was already interested might be to miss out on some terrific place. After all, how a college treats homeschoolers says a great deal about how they view education in general, and how comfortable the student would be there.

So I determined to go ahead and make a site that would, I hoped, function as the Peterson's for homeschoolers. I composed an email asking a few questions (What do you do about transcripts? Teacher recommendations? Do you change anything else about the admissions process and/or hold homeschoolers to higher standards?) and sent it off, at various times throughout the rest of my college career, to the majority of colleges in the country. Fewer than half, I'd say, responded. Those who did, often made it clear, by assuming I was a prospective student, that they hadn't so much as read my first sentence. A number of replies were downright cavalier, not to mention poorly punctuated (if at all) and ungrammatical. My favorite, though, was the college that had tossed my email around from one member of the admissions office to another. I did eventually receive a reply, but in scrolling down I saw how many tries it had taken for someone to come up with an answer and the bewilderment my questions had caused. It was then when I finally realized I'd had no cause to worry myself sick when I was looking at colleges; it was the places that knew the least that were the harshest.

I was even more interested to compare the replies I received from the colleges (who usually, as I've said, thought I was a prospective student) with their responses to the HSLDA survey on college admission policies and the occasional online list of homeschool-friendly colleges. Responses to surveys that would be posted on the web and generate free publicity elicited often quite different responses than casual replies to a real 'student.' Indeed, the

After Homeschool
Fifteen Homeschoolers Out In The Real World

by Anna Peak

perceived casualness of the whole endeavor sometimes led to luxuriant opinion mouthing. The dean at Kalamazoo College was one such; when I wrote back asking if I could post his reply verbatim, he sent back instructions on which sections I could use. However, what he had in fact done was not so much remove sections as re-write the email, eliminating the many dismissive or negative remarks he'd made about homeschoolers. Ironically, this time around he included my all-time favorite response: in listing things about K-College that might make homeschoolers a bad fit, he cited "an honor code that is open to interpretation." Indeed.

Nonetheless, American colleges and universities compared very favorably to colleges in Canada and the UK. Very little information is available to homeschoolers in those countries—not surprisingly, as homeschooling is relatively new there and the UK's Ofsted (Office of Standards in Education) makes unconventional educational routes exceedingly difficult. Some colleges I emailed literally had no idea what I was talking about when I mentioned home education (as they call it in the UK). Now they know.

As much as my site serves to provide basic information otherwise unavailable (and to act as a 'check-and-balance' to other sources of information), it also helps to inform the colleges on the other end of the process and occasionally even inspire change. For instance, the admissions staff at my alma mater, Rosemont, was thrown into a dither one day when they received a call from a prospective homeschooler—the first such inquiry since my call years before. The admissions office called the president of the college for instructions, and the president turned to the web manager and asked for advice. The web manager, it so happens, is a fellow alumna and my best friend, and has had to listen to me pontificate on the subject more than once. She was able to show my site to the president, who passed it on. The girl enrolled and admissions decided that for future, it would be best to have a counselor who specialized in dealing with homeschoolers. When, therefore, I emailed the president my senior year suggesting that someone write an official homeschool admissions policy, I met with a swift and enthusiastic response, and the homeschool coun-

Homeschoolers and College

selor and I did, in fact, sit down and write such a policy. Furthermore, I was asked for a number of suggestions on how best to actively recruit homeschoolers and many of those suggestions are currently being implemented.

More and more colleges are writing homeschool admissions policies, and a few are actively recruiting homeschoolers. The legal changes mentioned earlier are beginning to find their complement in an alteration in colleges' attitudes. Because the situation is in such a state of flux, it's essential that a homeschooler double-check on a college's homeschool admissions requirements. Those requirements, if any, change all the time, and then again they may in fact be more (or less) flexible than they appear, depending as much on staff turnover as anything else. It's usually best to ask to speak with the director of admissions, who has more knowledge and power regarding these issues than anyone (and who can even make up a policy for you on the spot, if need be); once you explain why you wish to speak with the director rather than a counselor, you will usually be transferred quickly.

In terms of choosing colleges to speak to, obviously I would recommend my own site (www.homeschoolersguide.tk), but there are several other sites out there with information on homeschoolers and college—a search on Google.com will turn up all of them, and the more information you have, the better off you are. In general colleges that are unusual or outstanding in some way are much more likely to welcome homeschoolers and particularly unschoolers. Particularly accepting are Ivy League and similar-caliber colleges; those with unusual curricula; women's colleges; very religious or liberal colleges; colleges that don't require SATs or grades, such as Evergreen State College, are all good general places to start.

After Homeschool
Fifteen Homeschoolers Out In The Real World

by Anna Peak

For some specific starting points, here is a list of my top 25 homeschooler-friendly colleges in alphabetical order.

1. Alverno College, WI
2. Amherst College, MA
3. Bates College, ME
4. Brown University, RI
5. Bucknell University, PA
6. California Institute of Technology
7. Cornell University, NY
8. Eastern University, PA
9. Harvard University, MA
10. Haverford College, PA
11. Hillsdale College, MI
12. Houghton College, NY
13. Huntingdon College, AL
14. Marlboro College, VT
15. Oral Roberts University, OK
16. Reed College, OR
17. Rosemont College, PA
18. St. John's College, MD and NM
19. Sarah Lawrence College, NY
20. Stanford University, CA
21. Swarthmore College, PA
22. Thomas Aquinas College, CA
23. Thomas More College of Liberal Arts, NH
24. Trinity College, CT
25. University of New Hampshire

Appendix

RESOURCES

Books

Tamra B. Orr

A Parent's Guide to Homeschooling: The Complete Guide

Grace Llewellyn

The Teenage Liberation Handbook: How to Quit School and Get a Real Life and Education

Real Lives: 11 Teenagers Who Don't Go to School

Cafi Cohen

And What About College?: How Homeschooling Can Lead to Admissions to the Best Colleges and Universities

Homeschoolers' College Admissions Handbook: Preparing your 12- to 18-Year Old for a Smooth Transition

Homeschooling: The Teen Years

Others

Cool Colleges for the Hyper-Intelligent, Self-Direction, Late Blooming and Just Plain Different, Donald Asher.

The Guidance Manual for the Christian Home School: A Parent's Guide for Preparing Home School Students for College or Career, David and Laurie Callihan

Homeschooling for Excellence, David and Micki Colfax

The Homeschoolers' Guide to Portfolios and Transcripts, Loretta Heuer

Home Learning Year by Year: How to Design a Homeschool Curriculum from Preschool through High School, Rebecca Rupp

A Sense of Self: Listening to Homeschooled Adolescent Girls, Susannah Sheffer

After Homeschool
Fifteen Homeschoolers Out In The Real World

Appendix

Websites

www.cis.upenn.edu/%7ebrada/homeschooling.html: A site created by a homeschooler about the different elements that go into home-schooling through the high school years.

paradoxical.nbtsc.org/schoolfree/: A site run by the teens who attend Grace Llewellyn's Not Back to School Camp.

www.nbtsc.org/wiki/NBTSWikiWiki: This web site tells you all about NBTSC itself.

www.apricotpie.com/: Written for homeschoolers by homeschoolers. Full of essays, poems and other thoughts on homeschooling and other topics.

members.tripod.com/~homeplanet98/index.html: An ICQ chatroom started specifically for homeschoolers.

www.gomilpitas.com/homeschooling/explore/teensites.htm: Addresses almost every homeschooling subject there is and has set-aside an area for teen's essays, questions and other information.

www.eatbug.com: Although apparently no longer maintained, this site created by a homeschooling teen has lots of fun things to read about homeschooling—prepare to chuckle.

Resources

AUTHOR BIOGRAPHY

Tamra Orr is a full time writer living in Portland, Oregon. She is the author of more than two dozen nonfiction books for children and families, including *250 Things Homeschoolers can do on the Internet* (Scarecrow Education), *A Parents Guide to Homeschooling: The Complete Guide* (Parents Guide Press) and *101 Ways to Make Your Library Homeschooling Friendly* (Mars Publishing). More importantly, she is the homeschooling mother of Jasmine (19), Nicole (12), Caspian (10) and Coryn (7), as well as wife of 21 years to life partner, Joseph. Orr received her bachelor's degree in English and Secondary Education from Ball State University in 1982 and believed everything the college taught her until she became a mother. Fortunately, her children set her on a better and truer pathway, which ended up leading, among other things, to homeschooling. She lived in northern Indiana all of her life, until 2001, when she and her family were fortunate enough to move to Oregon. In her four and a half spare minutes a day, Orr likes to read novels, snuggle with her children, talk to her husband and take a shower. Sometimes she has to do all four simultaneously if she wants to get them done. She welcomes comments, which may be sent to the publisher.

**parent's
guide
press**

P.O. Box 461730
Los Angeles, CA 90046
800.549.6646
323.782.1775 fax

A Parent's Guide to
Homeschooling

Author: Tamra B. Orr
Category: Parenting / Education
Format: Trade Paperback
ISBN: 1-931199-09-4
Pub Date: June 2002
Pages: 336
Price: $22.95 (CAN$34.95)
Trim: 7.375 x 9.125

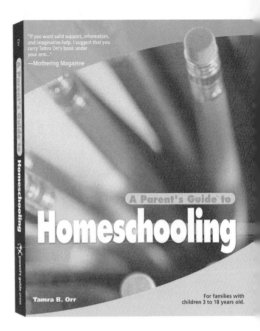

Expert Answers to Tough
Questions about Homeschooling

▶ **What families considering homeschooling need most**: answers to their questions. From the basic ("How did the movement begin?) to the devilish ("What about unhappy grandparents and other relatives?"), this collection of common questions and informed answers lead readers to the information they need, when they need it.

▶ *A Parent's Guide to Homeschooling* **features contributions from the foremost experts** in the field, including: Mark and Helen Hegener, founders of *Home Education Magazine*; Patrick Farenga, President of 'ohn Holt & Associates; Linda Dobson, author of *The Art of Education: Reclaiming Your Family, Community ᵈ Self*, among others; and Dr. Pat Montgomery Founder and Director of Clonlara School.

᠁e end of each chapter are one or more first-hand accounts from everyday homeschoolers.
the Trenches" essays share 'average homeschooler's' successes and failures, concerns and
These essays offer an additional perspective to topics covered by Tamra's Q&A and the
᠁utions.

᠁provides a snapshot of the legal requirements homeschoolers face in each of the fift
᠁ct info for support groups in each state. The appendix contains an analysis of the legal
᠁anada's provinces, written by Canadian homeschool pioneer and former Canadian
᠁riesnitz.

᠁ost important resources noted in the book, including support group contact
᠁ide Web resources, and important books, magazines, and journals.

᠁ted in the appendix, including books, journals, and magazines, an
᠁urces, and contact information for special interest homeschooling